T0255390

Building a Game Pitch

Based on the PocketGamer MasterClass *Building a Pitch: From Concept to Document* (2021), a decade's worth of industry experience and numerous industry-level pitches for a variety of organisations, including Mediatonic, Epic Games and GDC, this book will equip you with methodologies, best practices and insights around video game pitch design. It will guide you through a step-by-step process from initial conceptualisation and idea validation to communicating your pitches on paper clearly and effectively – as well as illustrating why such a process can be highly valuable.

In a day and age where video game development is more competitive than ever, the value and importance of "lightning in a bottle" pitches has never been higher: foundational visions capable of delivering video games that stand apart from the crowd as industry-renowned titles, generating immense critical or commercial success which (after the awe has abated) usually triggers the same internal question – "why didn't I think of that!?" As such, this book will cover:

- How video game pitches can determine the success potential of a video game
- How to conceptualise unique and compelling ideas for a video game
- How to validate your ideas to better determine whether they are capable of becoming "lightning in a bottle" experiences – or even worth prototyping
- How to structure, format and write a video game pitch in a manner that not only helps you better expand upon and understand your own pitch but also makes it easier for others to understand and buy into

This book will be of great interest to both seasoned and early-career game designers, students studying game design courses and start-up founders seeking investment.

Arran Topalian is currently Lead Designer at Oxalis Games Ltd., UK, with industry experience across studios such as Rare Ltd., Microsoft Research Cambridge and Mediatonic/Epic Games.

Building a Game Pitch
How to Bottle Lightning

Arran Topalian

CRC Press
Taylor & Francis Group
Boca Raton   London   New York

CRC Press is an imprint of the
Taylor & Francis Group, an **informa** business

Designed cover image: © Getty Images, Caia Image

First edition published 2024
by CRC Press
2385 NW Executive Center Drive, Suite 320, Boca Raton FL 33431

and by CRC Press
4 Park Square, Milton Park, Abingdon, Oxon, OX14 4RN

CRC Press is an imprint of Taylor & Francis Group, LLC

© 2024 Arran Topalian

ISBN: 978-1-032-21707-9 (hbk)
ISBN: 978-1-032-21701-7 (pbk)
ISBN: 978-1-003-26963-2 (ebk)

DOI: 10.1201/9781003269632

Typeset in Times New Roman
by Apex CoVantage, LLC

Contents

Preface

During my decade-long career in the games industry, I have written hundreds if not thousands of pages of design documentation – from proposals and specifications to countless pitch documents for various studios or clients. I am uncertain if that is a lot or a little by industry standards but, regardless, it has taught me just how powerful and important well-executed documentation can be when it comes to game design. Not to mention the value of a sturdy keyboard.

I appreciate that, in a day and age where game-creation tools are more plentiful and accessible than ever before, advocating design documentation might be a controversial or even boring point of view! Who wants to write design documentation of any sort when you could just jump right into an engine and start making something work in a bid to create the next hugely successful video game? Assuming, of course, that this is your goal – which is by no means the only reason to develop video games.

My hope is that, by reading this book, you will come to understand, appreciate and harness the value of a specific design document that I firmly believe can determine the success of a video game long before it is even playable: the video game pitch. A document whose importance and function could best be likened to the ground floor of a building – the foundational layer of a larger creation whose strength and shape inescapably determines what can be built upon it. A document which could maybe even help you change the world.

> You have the power to change the world. . . . Deep inside of you, every single one of you has the most powerful device known to man – and that's an idea. A single idea from the human mind, it could start a groundswell; it could be a flashpoint for a movement.

And it can actually rewrite our future. But an idea is powerless if it stays inside of you.

–Nancy Duarte[1]

NOTE

1. https://sw-ke.facebook.com/TEDxQueensVillage/videos/nancy-duarte/741489329665880/

Acknowledgements

Before we get started, I would like to thank everyone who has encouraged, empowered, supported or taken a chance on me throughout my career, including Dr Thomas Munck, Dr Dayna Galloway, Dr Iain Donald, Frank Arnot, Mike Chapman, Richard Banks and Tork Shaw – to name just a few. I would also like to thank CRC Press and Will Bateman for reaching out to me back in 2021 and asking if I would be interested in writing a book. It still hasn't sunk in.

I would also like to thank Indigo Levy for all her grammar corrections, proof-readings, reminders to eat something and insisting I do some writing whenever I procrastinated – which was often . . .

But most of all I would like to thank my inspirational mother, who bought me my first ever video game console, read out the dialogue with me as I played *Final Fantasy 7*, taught me the importance of pursuing what made me happiest and frequently kicked my butt at *Street Fighter* by mashing all the buttons and refusing to play properly.

Chapter 1

Introduction

1.1 THE TRANSFORMATIVE POWER OF BOTTLED LIGHTNING

An Italian plumber that jumps. A blue hedgehog that runs fast. A procedurally generated gameworld comprised of interactive blocks. A battle royale that revolves around construction. A series of variously sized falling bricks that can be slotted together in order to clear them. A kid-friendly third-person shooter that uses paint instead of bullets. A crowbar-toting scientist. I could go on!

There are some video games that manage to stand out from the crowd and become industry-renowned titles capable of transforming a studio overnight, turning into hugely successful IPs and oftentimes household names that generate immense critical and financial success for all involved which, in my experience (after the awe has abated), usually trigger the same internal question: "why didn't I think of that!?" Video games born from what I now refer to as "Commercially Viable Concepts" (CVCs) – a.k.a. lightning in a bottle!

Throughout my career I became increasingly obsessed with attempting to understand whether CVCs (which we will elaborate on further in the following chapters) shared some set of principles that might explain their success. A golden ratio of video game design that, once identified, could allow me to design video games of said calibre both reliably and consistently when applied. This obsession ultimately led me to learning about the value and significance of video game pitches and the art of "vision-crafting" within the creative process of game design – and in turn how to write a video game pitch effectively through literally dozens of professional pitch documents. This value and significance was made particularly apparent to me during my time at Mediatonic when *Fall Guys: Ultimate Knockout* first began circulating around the

DOI: 10.1201/9781003269632-1

studio after being pitched by a colleague. Despite being nothing more than several pages that captured the concept on paper, it was immediately apparent to both myself and the wider company that the game was something special, so much so that it was quickly invested in and developed into the smash-hit it is today. Witnessing this firsthand further reinforced my fascination with pitch documents and the belief that they were the key to creating CVCs.

It is these years' worth of learnings that I intend to share with you in this book: the video game development equivalent of how to measure twice in order to cut once – likeable to the old adage:

> If I had five minutes to chop down a tree, I'd spend the first three sharpening my axe.
>
> – Abraham Lincoln[1]

This front-loaded 'sharpening' is very much what I consider video game pitches to be – the process of setting yourself up for success well before you start swinging – so think of this book as a guide on how to sharpen your proverbial axe!

It goes without saying that you certainly do not need to agree with the opinions of this book, nor do you need to follow the processes it outlines, in order to make a successful video game – "successful" being defined by this book as achieving either commercial and/or critical acclaim. It is also worth noting, again, that this book does not intend to suggest that this goal is the be-all-and-end-all of video game development. But assuming this *is* indeed your goal, it is my hope that the contents of this book will arm you with the same knowledge that has allowed me to successfully conceptualise and communicate CVCs to numerous industry giants. As someone who has happily dedicated most of their life to playing countless CVC-level video games and has many fond memories involving them, the prospect of you or anyone else using this knowledge to create new CVCs that I myself might enjoy playing would make this designer very happy indeed!

This is not to say that a video game pitch can or should wholesale replace other available means of proving out an initial concept – such as prototyping. Jumping straight into a game engine to start knocking something together is a perfectly valid approach and definitely not an approach this book seeks to discourage or disparage. We all have different ways of solving problems and tapping into our creativity – what works for one may not work for another. I am also not trying to suggest that a video game pitch will solve all your future development problems! As I am sure anyone with any industry experience can attest to, making successful games is often the culmination of hard work, trust, collaboration and nothing short of ironcad determination from all involved. A little bit of smart marketing never hurts either.

However, much like the unseen and all-important foundations of an iceberg, while the pitch itself may never see the light of day, if used and executed correctly I would argue that it can play a vital and often severely underestimated role in determining a video game's potential for success before even a single line of its code has been written, as well as better ensuring uptake and buy-in in order to bring it to life. TL;DR I am of the firm belief that a game's concept and pitch-level design can be one of the biggest factors in determining its success or failure.

When trying to communicate their utility and value to others I have often compared a strong video game pitch to be much like a set of coordinates for a treasure map: derivable information that allows you to not only determine where to spend time and money *digging* – but also clearly communicate this location to others (see Figures 1.1 – 1.4).

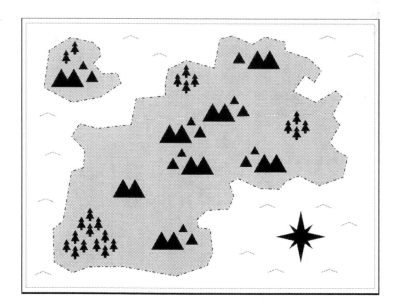

Figure 1.1 Design coordinates (A).

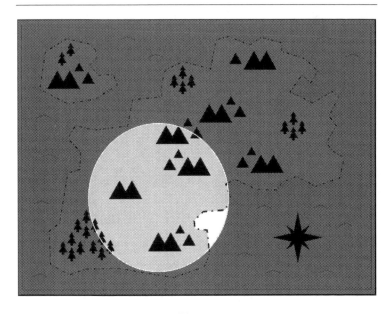

Figure 1.2 Design coordinates (B).

Figure 1.3 Design coordinates (C).

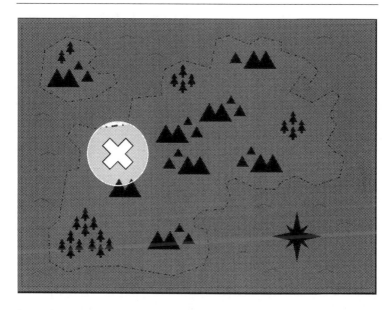

Figure 1.4 Design coordinates (D).

When you start out, you'll likely have little to no sense of these coordinates whatsoever, but over time, you'll begin to narrow in on that coveted X marks the spot.

The stronger the pitch, the more precise the coordinates you'll have and the less time, energy and money you'll have to spend digging everywhere looking for treasure.

1.2 ABOUT ME

I think it is safe to say that, from an early age, I devoted most of my life to Play.

My fascination with the act of play aside – from why we do it to its vital role in our development as humans – my relationship with play has been a constant throughout my life. Growing up, my parents always gave the same advice when it came to deciding what I wanted to do:

> Whether it's emptying trash-bins or designing rocket ships, do whatever you find the most fun, because when you're having fun, you're not working – you're playing.
>
> – Mum[2]

I suppose I took their advice rather literally in the end . . .

Ever since I got my hands on a *Sega Mega Drive*™ (thanks again Santa) for my third Christmas it was love at first sight. I played every game I could get my hands on which, as it happened, coincided rather nicely with what I personally consider to be the golden era of video gaming. Before long the first *Mario* dropped, *Sonic* was on the rise and with the *GameBoy*™ just around the corner, I quickly became – and I use this word quite intentionally – obsessed with video games and the countless experiences they could offer. An obsession that I can safely say continues to this very day, which both my Gamerscore/ Trophy-count can attest to and I now share with a distinct sense of both pride and reluctance for fear of looking like I never go out.[3] Which I totally, totally do . . .

While this childhood of games, spanning a wide array of shapes and sizes, may have taught me more about game design than I'm able to consciously remember, it somehow failed to teach me what I wanted to do with my life. At the time, the concept of further education in video games, be it their design or development, was unthinkable – let alone well surfaced. So when high school ended, I panicked and just picked an educational subject I had always enjoyed studying: History. It wasn't until four years and one hastily written dissertation later (I apologise here and now to whoever had to read that) during a voluntary placement at a high school that I realised if I were to keep walking down that road, it would become harder and harder to turn back. I asked myself if being a History teacher was really what I, personally, wanted to be waking up to for the rest of my life.

The answer, as I am sure you can guess by now, was no – it was not. Fast-forward a couple years of working in retail and call centres to save up some money, I funded myself through a second degree at Abertay Dundee University in Game Design & Production Management, leading to positions at companies such as Rare, Microsoft Research Cambridge, Oculus and Mediatonic which (somehow) got me to where I am today – writing a book about video game pitches.

When I first sat down to write this book, I promised myself this particular section would be as brief as possible. 'Who in their right mind wants to read anything about me?', I asked myself. But re-reading it, followed by the usual pause as I consider whether to delete the entire section, my hope is that it offers someone out there who is currently in the position I once was a little bit of much-needed reassurance. If working in the games industry is something you truly want to do: keep going. Keep playing games that bring you joy. Keep making games that showcase your passion. Perhaps even games whose designs follow the advice and practices outlined in this book – so feel free to take it with you on your journey. It can, after all, be dangerous to go alone.

1.3 ABOUT YOU

Take a look at the intentionally exhaustive list here:

- 'I want to learn how a video game pitch could help me develop a successful game . . . '
- 'I want to learn what an industry-level video game pitch should look like or contain . . . '
- 'I want to make a video game – but I can't come up with an idea for what I should make . . . '
- 'I have an idea for a video game I would like to make – but I am not sure if it is worth developing further . . . '
- 'I have an idea for a video game I would like to make which I am fairly confident is worth developing further – but I am not sure how to validate it . . . '
- 'I have an idea for a video game I would like to make that I am very confident is worth developing further – but I am not sure how to do that . . . '
- 'I have an idea for a video game I would like to make that I am very confident is worth developing further which I fully understand – but I am not sure how to explain it to others without them falling asleep or getting confused . . . '

If any of the above sounds like you, to some degree or another, then you are in the right place!

1.4 ABOUT THIS BOOK

Whenever I am writing any form of design documentation, be it a pitch or otherwise, I typically begin (in one form or another) by explaining exactly what the purpose of the document is. This can not only help readers understand the overall goal of a document and ensure they are aware of what to expect, but also ensure they can determine whether the document is relevant to their needs – which is ironically a topic that lies at the very heart of the process this book will be covering. Not to mention the fact that it can be easy for the writer to lose sight of the solution they are trying to outline if they don't first fully understand or are able to quickly recall the problem they are trying to solve.

So that is exactly what I am going to do now!

The purpose of this book is to offer the sum total of my own opinions, knowledge and experience around creating video game pitches and, as such, is intended to offer you – dear reader – the following key learnings:

1. How video game pitches can determine the success potential of a video game
2. How to conceptualise unique and compelling ideas for a video game
3. How to validate your ideas to better determine whether they are capable of becoming CVCs
4. How to structure, format and write a video game pitch in a manner that not only helps you better expand upon and understand your own pitch but also makes it easier for others to understand and buy into

This book, in short, is a step-by-step framework derived from my personal experiences around video game pitching and subsequent design for anyone who wants the next video game they develop to have a higher chance of being successful via the process of vision-crafting.

To achieve this goal, this book has been divided into three main chapters, each of which is composed of several clearly titled sub-chapters, so if you are looking for help with a specific part of the process then you will (hopefully) know where to look!

While the content of this book cannot 100% guarantee that your video game will be a CVC, I can certainly guarantee that everything I have included in this book has proven to be incredibly effective for several of my own industry-level video game pitches across indie to AAA clients, not only resulting in increased interest and investment from industry professionals or potential stakeholders, but also setting projects up for success through a well-considered foundation and clearer sense of direction. I will also endeavour to keep this book as concise and easy-to-follow as I possibly can to provide an almost *paint-by-numbers* approach to video game pitch design that offers you every best practice and pitfall heads-up that I have learned and benefitted from throughout my decade in the games industry when it comes to video game pitches.

NOTES

1. https://quoteinvestigator.com/2014/03/29/sharp-axe/
2. Hey, Mum – love you!
3. As of 26 May 2023: 150,123 Gamerscore | 351 PS Trophies (in case you were wondering)

Chapter 2

Conceptualisation

2.1 CHAPTER INTRODUCTION

We currently live in an unprecedented era of video game development where free-to-use game engines and a vast volume of learning material online have made it easier than ever to develop and deploy fully functioning video games. But with this accessibility comes a more competitive industry than ever before. Standing out from this larger-than-ever crowd can take significant time and money, making game development a (sometimes sizeable) gamble, so anything that can improve the odds of placing a safe bet is surely a positive!

In my opinion, this makes the conceptualisation phase of video game development more critical than ever before, which involves generating, validating, expanding upon and clearly understanding the core concept that forms the foundation of any video game's design. By giving this phase the attention it deserves, you can create a solid foundation for your video game that I believe can greatly increase the chances of its success in the marketplace.

While the saying, '10% is the idea and 90% is the execution', may hold true in terms of the time and effort required for developing something, when it comes to value, I would argue that the initial 10% can sometimes be more valuable than the remaining 90%, especially when it comes to video game development. For instance, a gemstone in a piece of jewellery may only account for a very small percentage of the complete piece, but could also be the most valuable part! While execution is undoubtedly essential, even the best-executed video games will struggle to find an audience if the underlying idea is weak, uninspired or poorly thought-through.

To illustrate this point, consider the foundation of a building which, despite only being a small percentage of the overall structure, is

DOI: 10.1201/9781003269632-2

undeniably the most critical component since everything else depends on it. Similarly, the early stages of developing a video game – i.e., conceptualisation and ideation – are crucial in that they lay the foundation for the rest of the game's development. If there is a flaw or inherent restriction in the foundation, it is usually only a matter of time until it is felt in the upper floors and may even drastically limit what can be created. Therefore, it is essential to give these initial stages of game development – the formation of its foundation – the attention it deserves in order to maximise the chances of conceiving a CVC.

But if we are to stand a chance of creating a CVC, we first need to firmly understand exactly what a CVC is.

2.2 DEFINING CVCs

I would argue "good design" ultimately hinges on how well a product fulfils the needs and wants and of its intended audience, whether it is a car, a meal or even a video game.

With the latter in mind, I define a CVC primarily as a video game capable of catering to a large enough group of previously uncatered for players who share either one or several unmet needs (see Figure 2.1) and satisfies each rung of the Lightning Rod – which we will be covering later in this book.

However, it is important to note that a game's popularity or player count does not always correlate with its design quality or innovation – just as a restaurant's popularity doesn't always guarantee good food! As an avid gamer, I myself have played many video games that brought me joy but did not achieve or seem to seek CVC status. As mentioned earlier, attempting to create a CVC is far from the only goal of video game development, but it can certainly be a game-changer for a studio's success – whether it happens unexpectedly or by design.

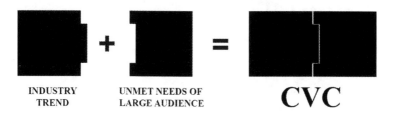

INDUSTRY   **UNMET NEEDS OF**   **CVC**
TREND   **LARGE AUDIENCE**

Figure 2.1 Primary components of a CVC.

Now that we have further defined what a CVC is, the next question is how to create one as part of the vision-crafting process, which begins with the origin-point of any good bolt of lightning: a Spark.

2.3 THE SPARK

At the heart of every potential CVC, as illustrated in Figure 2.2, resides what I like to call a *Spark* – which comes well before the full pitch and longer still before the video game itself and is formed as part of a video game's conceptualisation.

Figure 2.2 The Spark.

It took me a while to articulate what, exactly, the Spark is! While it was something I unconsciously understood and appreciated the importance of when writing pitches of my own, I had never attempted to consciously define or describe, at least until I sat down to write this book.

The Spark, simply put, is the very core of your video game: something forged from our soon-to-be-discussed conceptualisation methodologies while considering the also soon-to-be-discussed limitations of our design restrictions – the hammer and anvil of vision-crafting which when combined create, well, Sparks! It is from this seed that a video game's entire experience evolves and in my opinion ultimately determines whether a video game could become a CVC, regardless of how pretty it may end up looking, or even how fun it may end up feeling to play.

This is not to say that a Spark is the same thing as a mere idea, which are by comparison sporadic, extremely vague and without forethought, making them highly risky and relatively valueless. Think of a Spark as medication chosen for a specific diagnosis and think of an idea as medication simply chosen at random – an overall negative and unwise approach for everyone involved. It is also not to say that a Spark is the same thing as a full video game design, which can take several years and countless other design documents to comprehend; nor is it a fully written video game pitch wherein this core concept has been expanded upon.

Now – let's take a closer look at that anvil.

2.4 DESIGNING BY RESTRICTION

You may be wondering why the first thing we are going to discuss about the highly creative process of idea generation is to do with restriction – surely restrictions are the last thing we want at this point! But as anyone who has ever been faced with a blank sheet of paper can confirm, infinite possibilities can be extremely intimidating and very unhelpful, in that we have no way of knowing where to even start. You may also find that restrictions are remarkably effective at breeding innovation – or to put it another way:

Necessity is the mother of invention.

– Plato[1]

While the possibilities of that blank sheet of paper in front of you may seem endless, there is not as much empty space on that page as you might think, which can make life much easier when conceptualising.

To use an admittedly flowery analogy: if an idea is a painting, composed of an infinite range of potential colours and usage, then our restrictions are what come beforehand – namely:

1. Knowing what kind of canvas we are able to paint on
2. Knowing what size of canvas we are able to paint on
3. Knowing what colours of paint we are able to paint with

To better illustrate my point: when you have a moment, put this book down and look up any car that you like before asking yourself if the design of that car on your screen is a good design. Chances are that it is a fairly impossible question to answer – or at least it should be! This is because it is impossible to determine how "good" a design is without first knowing what or whose problems the design is attempting to solve. It is these problems that are just one of several types of restriction that we ideally need to identify first and foremost before putting pen to paper.

This is why understanding what our restrictions are before anything else is so vitally important and where my own creative process when it comes to video game pitches typically begins: they can help us narrow in on what concepts to even humour. Think of every restriction as an imagination filter of sorts: a series of nets that exist between your magnificent mind and that empty sheet of paper which your idea must pass through in order to qualify for further consideration (see Figure 2.3).

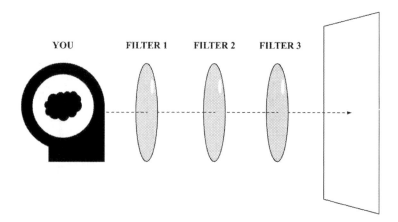

Figure 2.3 Designing by restriction.

Pitching the biggest and best game design in the world is all well and good but if, for example, you could never have the resources required to make it, that pitch is surely not one worth pursuing as-is given its necessities and subsequent restrictions. In short: it is always important to temper creativity with feasibility and purpose.

In the past, I have sometimes received what is called an RFP – or Request For Pitch. These are essentially creative briefs from potential clients requesting specific pitches that must, for whatever business-related reason or otherwise, adhere to several criteria. This concept is a perfect example of a clear, concise set of restrictions – the only difference being someone else has taken the time to identify and communicate what they are! For example:

> We are looking to develop a casual mobile title about cats that can compete with games such as [insert major casual mobile game here]. The product should take no longer than a year to develop, appeal to a broad audience and may support a 5–10 person team.
> – Imaginary Client

Upon closer inspection, there are several clear restrictions throughout this imaginary RFP that we can identify, which have been peeled out and broken down in Table 2.1.

> We are looking to develop a *casual, mobile* title about *cats*. The product should take no longer than *a year to develop, appeal to a broad audience* and may support a *5–10 person team*.

Table 2.1 Imaginary RFP – Restrictions Breakdown

Criteria	Restriction
Casual	The design cannot require a high skill barrier
Mobile	The design cannot feature too many commands
Cats	The design cannot fail to feature cats
A year to develop	The design cannot be too big in terms of scope
Appeal to a broad audience	The design cannot be overly mature or gory
5–10 person team	The design cannot depend on a large workforce

So before you start thinking about what abilities your video game will have or where your video game will transport players to, take some time to first ask yourself what your restrictions are, because I guarantee you will find them to be far friendlier than a blank sheet of paper. Your restrictions may even lead you to previously inconceivable concepts or ingenious solutions that become iconic strengths! For instance, *Minecraft*'s unique art style partly emerged from practical considerations – that is, restrictions – regarding the limited processing power of computers at the time of its development, so the game's creator (Markus Notch Persson) intentionally chose a blocky, low-resolution art style to make the game easier to run on older hardware.

To offer you some real examples of restrictions I have set myself in the past for a specific pitch:

- 'The game I want to pitch must be mass multiplayer'
- 'The game I want to pitch must be easy for children to play'
- 'The game I want to pitch must offer a light, friendly gameworld to exist in'
- 'The game I want to pitch must offer endless replayability'

Each of these restrictions helped me narrow down the otherwise infinite range of creative possibilities by ruling out certain options – it is much easier to find a needle in a haystack once you start removing some of the hay!

When it comes to specifying your own restrictions, I recommend outlining some answers for at least five Key Restrictions, each of which I myself almost always consider when building a video game pitch from scratch well before ideation begins.

2.4.1 Key Restriction #1: Opportunity

This initial and critical restriction revolves around identifying a substantial unmet need in the video game market capable of leveraging an industry trend while also innovating or enhancing it.

> You've got to start with the customer [their problems & requirements] . . . and work backwards to the technology. You can't start with the technology and try to figure out where you're going to try to sell it.
>
> – Steve Jobs[2]

Let's use Mediatonic's *Fall Guys: Ultimate Knock-out* as an example to help explain this key restriction a little further. At a pitch level, this particular video game took the battle royale genre – an already popular and successful genre at the time of its development and release considering the likes of competitors such as *PUBG* or *Fortnite* – and combined it with both a style of gameplay and aesthetic that was far more approachable.

As a result, this allowed it to not only appeal to an already substantial pre-existing audience (i.e. an audience who already like and play battle royales) but also reach an even broader audience in younger players – thanks to said gameplay and visual style. Most importantly, however, is that in doing so, it offered parents a battle royale that they could play with their children without requiring superior hand-eye coordination – a previously unmet opportunity just waiting to be filled by the right video game. It offered something joyful and colourful rather than gritty and violent that was released at a time when this was precisely the kind of escape people needed!

Another prime example could be something like *Valheim*: a video game which took the already highly popular proc-gen open-world exploration, survival and creativity-infused home construction elements of *Minecraft*. By combining these elements with clearly surfaced long-term goal bosses, higher fidelity visuals and a maturer premise, I would argue that it offered a *Minecraft*-esque experience better suited for a hardcore audience who were clearly yearning for such a game. Another opportunity successfully fulfilled.

A third and final example that hopefully illustrates the point I'm attempting to convey is the mobile sensation *Among Us*: a social deduction video game wherein players cooperate to complete tasks while one of them secretly attempts to kill everybody else without their identity being discovered. This form of dynamic was, however, first introduced by Dmitry Davidoff's *Mafia* in 1986, which was further popularised by its subsequent board-game evolution, *Werewolf*.[3] I believe that where *Among Us* truly succeeded lay in its presentation and availability: providing an immensely popular, successful and effective game dynamic to a far broader audience via a visual style designed to attract said audience and a platform with worldwide reach and instantaneous multiplayer.

Looking for these sorts of opportunities will, more often than not, play a substantial role when designing by restriction.

When considering this particular key restriction, I have often found that it helps to imagine players as fish. Bear with me – I promise this is going somewhere! Not only do I imagine them as fish but, more importantly, I imagine that they each belong to one of many different species of fish, all with their own distinct appetites and populations. Your pitch is tantamount to fish bait: something composed of specific elements or ingredients that have been carefully chosen for attracting and "catching" a specific species based on their preferences and needs – or what they like to eat if you prefer. Some may enjoy consuming "bait" that is colourful and family-friendly, whereas others may prefer consuming what allows them to dominate others in contests of hand-eye coordination and response times. Regardless, your goal is to design a bait capable of attracting a species of player that is both very hungry and highly populated, who are just waiting for the right bait to come along.

Each boat in the diagram of Figure 2.4 represent existing video games of varying success – hence the different sizes – and the fish as players. If you are looking to create a CVC-level pitch I would personally advise one of the following options when it comes to identifying opportunities for a pitch:

1. A highly populated species of player that is not being overfished – i.e., players who are not already being more than well-catered for

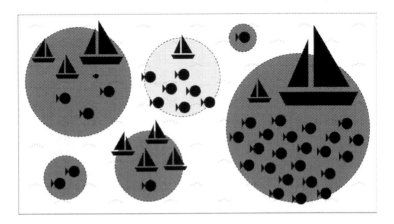

Figure 2.4 Hungry player-type volume versus Hungry player-type demand.

2. A highly populated species of player who may or may not be overfished but do have unfulfilled needs
3. An entirely new highly populated species of player that no existing video games are tapping into

I would argue that achieving one of these options is more often than not what the majority of successful CVCs accomplish.

What is also important to recognise is that some designs are capable of attracting species of players that are considerably more plentiful than others. This is what is often referred to in the industry as appeal or approachability, with broad appeal being a common buzz phrase and highly sought-after quality: games that can be played by as many potential players as possible. It stands to reason why games with broad appeal are highly prized: the more players that want to and can play your game, the greater the potential for commercial success – much like more foot traffic passing through a store leading to potentially higher revenue generated. This is especially the case in multiplayer games wherein players are essentially game content for other players – multiplayer games tend to not be very fun when there's no one else to play with! To offer an example, *Mario* was originally released in 1985[4] and since then has seen many sequels which typically involve the same core ingredients: a friendly Italian plumber who must do lots of jumping, in progressively harder and varied ways, to beat the game. Considering the long-running success and exceptional popularity of the *Mario* franchise across several generations, this particular type of bait (consisting of a specific style of aesthetic; gameplay; mastery) is clearly very tasty – and very effective.

Furthermore, when looking for these opportunities, you should attempt to gauge how strong the given industry trend is – be it battle royale or otherwise. This trend strength, in addition to potential pre-existing audience size, can often be roughly determined simply by looking at the design and popularity of video games currently on the market. Which video games are immensely popular right now – and how long have they been around for? Which video games are being streamed the most despite being several months or even years old? It doesn't take in-depth analyses or costly analytics platforms to answer these sorts of questions – you don't need a crystal ball to know that something like *Minecraft* isn't going anywhere anytime soon! Remember that your pitch may take several years to actually make, so be sure to gauge whether the opportunity you are hoping to seize will still be

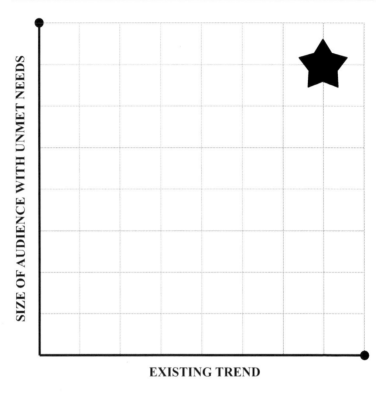

Figure 2.5 Opportunity axis

there by the time your pitch has been transformed into a playable video game.

In short: this restriction involves trying to gauge where your pitch might land on the graph illustrated in Figure 2.5. The higher it scores on both axes, the likelier it is that you have got a CVC on your hands!

To briefly elaborate a little further on the previous diagram: imagine that there are several great kids games on the market capable of attracting and maintaining large user-bases. One option would be to design your own potentially great kids game and go toe-to-toe with the competition in an attempt to poach their audience. Another option – the one I would advise – would be to consider if said competition wasn't satisfying certain requirements for the given audience. Maybe none of them allow for parents to play alongside their kids, or maybe all competing titles offer the same experience in terms of genre. Maybe none of them allow kids to play alongside their friends. Or maybe they would resonate with a different genre that harnesses what they seem to like about the competitors. It is a case of weighing up the estimated size of a target audience (based on existing video games) versus the quantity or severity of any unmet needs they may have.

2.4.2 Key Restriction #2: Intended Target Audience

Once you have identified a viable and valuable opportunity, it is even more important that you take the time to understand their likes, dislikes and behaviourisms.

First we strive to identify – then we seek to understand.

While studying game design at Abertay University, my tutors always advised considering the target audience of designs, which (to be totally honest with you) I didn't fully appreciate the importance of at the time. 'What difference does someone's age, gender or background have to do with the kind of games they like?', I would ask myself before disregarding the advice entirely in favour of designing whatever I thought sounded cool. I later found out that I had simply misunderstood the point of the exercise – and what design is ultimately all about.

A recent example of this that comes to mind involved my very own niece and nephew. I had been designing a children's card game, the main mechanic revolving around taking turns drawing cards from a pile, which I was confident would appeal to kids on several different levels – until I saw firsthand how young children actually play card-games. . . . I quickly learned that, while they might enjoy the theme, the role they were playing or even the general mechanics of my design, none of it mattered in the face of two children whose only interests lay in snatching as many cards as possible from the pile irrespective of whose turn it was! This, to their credit, was indeed a tremendous amount of fun – but such are the perils of designing for an audience whose needs and preferences are not fully identified or understood.

In short, the purpose of considering your intended target audience at this point in the process is to consider the possible needs and preferred skill sets (e.g. memory or hand-eye coordination) of those who will eventually play your game – something you should be thinking about from the earliest point possible. For instance, consider Nintendo's *New Super Mario Bros* and Maddy Makes Games' *Celeste*, two truly exceptional platformers. Visual styles aside, despite both of them being side-scrolling platformers, I would argue that they each play very differently precisely because they are intended for very different audiences – resulting in additional design differences because of this all-important distinction. For instance, where *New Super Mario Bros'* jump feels floaty, *Celeste's* feels comparatively snappier and while perhaps less suitable for younger audiences for whom the skill barrier is too high, is in turn better suited for a more hardcore platforming audience – further catered for with its multi-layered narrative and inclusion of dialogue.

Speaking of Nintendo, while writing this book they released an advertisement for their upcoming flagship title *Zelda: Tears of the Kingdom*, which revolves around a working middle-aged man who – through playing *Zelda* – finds the adventure and freedom he appears to miss in his day-to-day life. As this trailer (in my opinion) indicates, if there was ever a developer who understands the importance and success-defining power of knowing and designing for their target audience, it is Nintendo: a company whose designs continually focus on accessible depth and a crystal clear set of target audiences in mind.

It is important to understand that the term target audience needn't refer to a specific demographic group such as men aged 18–35. While this somewhat narrow definition of target audience is what I used to believe was important when it came to thinking about target audiences, it typically didn't prove to be very useful or even helpful, at least in my experience. I would highly recommend seeing them as groups of players who share characteristics or preferences in the video games they play in order to create more effective and engaging products or content. For example:

- Parents looking for games to play with their children
- Young couples interested in playing together
- Middle-aged working professionals who miss the magical possibilities of childhood imagination
- Players who enjoy decorating and customising instead of hand/eye-coordination focused experiences

It is also important to note that despite identifying a target audience, there is no guarantee that they will be the ones who will engage with your video game, hence my very intentional inclusion of the word 'intended' in this section's title. Metrics and time will ultimately reveal who, exactly, your game ends up attracting. But designing anything

without at least some sense of end-user in mind is akin to flying blind –
fun to begin but maybe not the wisest long-term plan!

2.4.3 Key Restriction #3: Scope

The term 'scope' relates to the amount of work that would be required
to create your pitch – from design documentation and code to art assets
or SFX. Literally anything that would be required to turn your pitch
into an actual video game.

For example, the video game *Pac-Man* would, by modern standards, be considered small in scope, in that it only requires a few simple
art assets (e.g. *Pac-Man* himself, the ghosts, the dots) and isn't overly
complex in terms of functionality. Conversely, something like the original *Mario* would (in comparison to *Pac-Man*) be much larger in scope,
considering all the art assets required to create the levels; the design of
the levels themselves; the different power-ups; developing and honing
the iconic *Mario* jump – to name just a few of the many tasks involved
in making something like *Mario*! All of these tasks take time not just
to conceptualise and understand but also, implement, prove out, test
and refine and as we all know – time costs money. So before you put
pen to paper, be sure to consider how much time you have available,
which will undoubtedly influence your creative options and the scope
of your pitch.

It is unlikely you or the team involved will manage to make the next
Call of Duty: Warzone if you only have six to twelve months of development time to play with . . .

2.4.4 Key Restriction #4: Resources

If someone was to task you with designing a building and all you had
available in terms of supplies were a couple planks of wood, a hammer
and some nails, it is unlikely you would start drawing up plans for the
Eiffel Tower 2.0 – and rightly so!

When it comes to game development, 'resources' include anything
you will realistically have access to when it comes to actually making your pitch, from funding, manpower and hardware to your own
personal skill set, pre-existing knowledge or even access to learning
materials.

It is important to carefully consider your resources before attempting
to conceptualise, as it can greatly help keep your wonderful imagination

in check and avoid you creating pitches that are quite simply beyond your means. That said, however limited your resources may be, do not despair! As we touched on before, your design restrictions are anything but shortcomings: they are strengths – each one providing a filter that I promise will breed ingenuity and innovation rather than constraint or limitation. The beauty of game design is that a lot can often be achieved with very little. Take Blanchot and Cottereau's *Dobble* as an example: a card-game whose only assets (beyond the fascinating and unseen maths that drives it) include dozens of circular cards dotted with relatively simple illustrations.[5] No fancy board to paint up. No finely detailed figurines to design, model and manufacture. Yet still once crowned the UK's biggest-selling card game – which isn't too bad for just fifty-five paper discs, a bit of maths and some very clever game design.[6]

One final bit of advice that I would like to offer when it comes to resources is to steal the authors' mantra: write what you know. To illustrate my point, consider Bungie's long-running *Destiny 2*, a free-to-play first-person shooter (FPS) which as of March 2023 boasts approximately forty-million subscriptions.[7] *Destiny 2* is the sequel to *Destiny*, which Bungie released in September 2014[8] after parting ways with *Microsoft* in 2007,[9] who originally acquired Bungie and its signature title *Halo* in 2000.[10] After spending several years designing and developing *Halo*, it is interesting to note that Bungie's next project was another FPS experience, rather than something completely different in terms of genre. As we mentioned beforehand – pre-existing knowledge is a valuable resource. Bungie had already learned how to make an FPS and what it took to make an FPS fun for a certain target audience – why waste it? To put it simply: when it came to their next project (*Destiny*) they clearly opted to write what they knew about.

That is not to say that if you have developed nothing but platformers you shouldn't try to branch out. It is only to say that, if you happen to know a lot about something already, be it how to develop an FPS, the anatomy of the human body, how the pieces of a gun fit together or how to climb a mountain, it is all a valuable resource – and something you could potentially put to very good use!

2.4.5   Key Restriction #5: Platform

Our fifth key restriction is relatively short, sweet and simple but still worth mentioning – especially if you are relatively new to game design or pitch creation!

The term 'platform' in this context relates to the device or devices you foresee your pitch being played on (e.g. PC, mobile, games console). Some platforms typically support certain types of video game experiences better than others, so it is an important restriction to consider during conceptualisation, from both experiential and commercial perspectives. Not only should your pitch complement its intended platform, whether for technical or gameplay reasons, but you should also consider how prevalent your intended target audience is on the given platform.

Video games from the fighter genre, as an example, typically involve a high volume of distinct player commands. This, in turn, usually requires either several button inputs or combining button inputs quickly and accurately. Because of this, one could argue that mobile devices may not be ideal for such a genre purely because such devices don't feature any tactile buttons or – as a result – enough haptic feedback to support the latter, unless your pitch intends to solve these platform-inherent drawbacks through its design . . . Hint, hint.

While there are typically workarounds that can rationalise or even excuse certain design decisions regardless of potential pitfalls – e.g., 'yes, but this pitch would still work on mobile if players owned a mobile gaming controller' – it is worth remembering that every *yes,* but your video game pitch relies on could be another red flag. It might sound minor on paper – a future problem for future you to solve – but failing to provide genuine answers to such questions misses the point of this entire process: to produce a well-thought-out pitch composed of decisions that are always infused with rationale. If such a question ever comes up that you cannot answer, or can only answer on the grounds of mere personal preference, consider the possibility that you might be chasing the wrong rabbit down the wrong rabbit hole.

2.5 CONCEPTUALISATION METHODOLOGIES

Now that we have outlined our restrictions we can finally move on to the second half of a Spark's coin: the high-level concept – i.e. the core experience of your video game.

For anyone unfamiliar with the term 'high-level', which is an important concept to understand given its relevance to video game pitches, I would like to offer you a quick analogy that will hopefully help! Imagine that there is a large river you wish to cross. The high-level aspect of solving this completely relatable and in no way ludicrous problem would first involve deciding how best to cross said river at a high level – such as building a bridge. However, just saying 'let's build a bridge' is not even nearly enough information to actually start building a bridge, which is where low-level information comes in for example:

- The materials needed to build the bridge
- Exactly how much of those materials are needed
- How those materials will be used

You will need to become familiar with moving along this spectrum of expression in order to write an effective game pitch – one that doesn't get too bogged down in details without (by contrast) becoming too vague either. Trying to explain everything at once and focusing too much on low-level information is easily the most common issue I have encountered when teaching or advising others on writing pitch documents. So if you are ever struggling to differentiate between the two later on, or indeed at any point, just remember: bridges!

For some people who have more ideas than they have time to make them all, the conceptualisation part is the easiest thing in the world. For others, this initial step can be the most frustrating, even if one's design restrictions help narrow things down. This section is primarily for the latter group, which will be covering several lengthily entitled conceptualisation methodologies, each offering different approaches to concept generation that have proven to be quite effective throughout my own career, in that they have typically produced good results in terms of the core experiences formed and resulting pitches or video games that have followed. That being said, the former group may still find these techniques helpful, specifically when it comes to ideation with the creation of CVCs in mind. They are by no means the only ways of approaching video game conceptualisation – far from it – but I have often found them to really help get the juices flowing and create clear, coherent, exciting and effective Sparks.

I should also point out that these approaches require varying levels of familiarity with already existing video games and media. The reason for this, pretentious as it admittedly may sound, is that (at least to my mind) being a game designer can be a bit like being a chef: the more knowledge you have about ingredients – the greater your creative options when cooking. In the game design sense of the word, ingredients span across a near infinite range of systems and mechanics, be it the ability to jump, how a jump feels in a specific game or how player progression (i.e. the in-game goals players strive to complete) is handled in another. Furthermore, just as a chef eats to broaden their palette, discover new ingredients and experience new ways of combining them to inspire combinations of their own, so too should a game designer play to achieve the same outcome. What better way to learn your ingredients – in terms of what does or doesn't work well together – than by consuming great experiences made by others! What can make game design particularly challenging in this regard, however, is that every-so-often some clever clogs will invent an entirely new ingredient, be it a mechanic, style of experience, progression system or monetisation approach. Long story short, the more familiar you are with design ingredients – countless though they may be – the greater your creative options will become. That certainly is not to say that you should "stay out of the kitchen" if you don't play many video games – only that I would recommend using the ingredients you are familiar with! It can be risky using an ingredient you don't know much about and aren't able or willing to put the required time into fully understanding it. That being said, if you are serious about designing video games, much like a chef would likely be remiss if they refused to broaden their palette by trying as many different cuisines as possible, I would highly encourage you to actually play video games. Play as many of them as you can. Understand what is important to different genres. What you like. What you think could be better – and why. It certainly isn't vital, but in my experience, this knowledge and familiarity can really make all the difference between a good pitch and a great one.

Before we jump into the conceptualisation methodologies themselves (we're nearly there) I would like to offer you some preliminary information around the similarity you will no doubt spot before long, which is that the majority of them essentially involve splicing pre-existing references together to produce new creations, because (as Arkane Creative Director Dinga Bakaba once put it) all video games are ultimately hybrids[11] – a sentiment further reinforced by industry heavyweights such as Naughty Dog:

> [We] wanted to take the character building and interaction of *Ico*
> and blend it with the tension and action of *Resident Evil 4*.[12]
>   – Ricky Cambier (*The Last of Us* designer)

Throughout my career, I have personally found this approach to be the most effective when it comes to conceptualisation, in terms of both design quality and helping others understand a pitch. As such, I would like to briefly outline what I believe Bakaba actually means!

As we have already covered, a video game's design could be equated to a cooking recipe, in the sense that its creation involves combining ingredients intended to complement each other, which in turn is intended to satisfy a particular consumer with particular preferences. There are three additional and equally important similarities that may be called out with this comparison in mind:

1. We can't simply throw stuff into the pot, cross our fingers and hope for the best
2. Certain ingredients inherently complement each other better than others, which is simply learned through experience and familiarity with them
3. Every recipe typically shares several key design aspects

Regarding the third and final point, just as aspects such as timing or seasonings are considerations almost every recipe needs to define, so too do video game designs. I call such concepts Prime Aspects (see Figure 2.6) – the fundamental realms of hybridisation which primarily include but are by no means limited to:

It should be noted that these are purely the aspects which I personally consider to be of prime level! There may very well be more, or different aspects that you or others consider to be of similar importance.

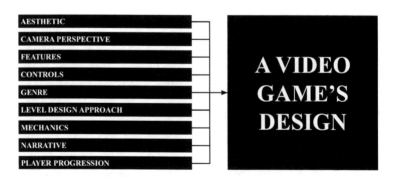

Figure 2.6 Prime Aspects.

With all of this in mind, circling back to Bakaba's quote about all video games being hybrids, I would argue that he is referring to the fact that many game designs essentially combine different Prime Aspects together to varying degrees. Some video games may simply blend two or more genres together whereas others may combine several Prime Aspects. For example, Naughty Dog's CVC *Uncharted* not only hybridises multiple genres – including platformer, third-person shooter and puzzler – but also couples them with various mechanics or features which are by no means new but complement the design, such as regenerating health and ammo reliance. This is most definitely not to say that this was how *Uncharted* was conceptualised – nor that *Uncharted's* design is unoriginal or simply a combination of pre-existing concepts – but more to highlight how combining these pre-existing elements can create a totally new experience.

After almost a decade in the video games industry, I can say with confidence that expressing concepts through the combination of existing references is incredibly commonplace, which stands to reason considering we are all surrounded by people who also play video games and understand the references! This, as we touched on beforehand, is all the more reason to acquaint yourself with as many game designs as possible. Trust me when I say that attempting to explain or understand a combat design, either verbally or on paper, is much harder than being able to point at an existing combat design that you or others can experience firsthand.

Now, without further ado, let's take a look at the conceptualisation methodologies I have found to be the most effective when attempting to write a new video game pitch!

2.5.1 The Razor

The Razor, as I like to call it, involves combining several design aspects, prime or otherwise, from two to four existing references – the "edges" of our Razor – in order to produce a high-level sense of this yet-to-be-made video game. Something that conveys not only intended gameplay but also any other important elements of its design that are vital to the experience – be it player count or even a specific form of meta progression.

I have often found that attempting to combine any more references than two to four usually leads to an overly complicated or confusing pitch that fails to create a clear picture in the mind's eye of the reader – but you are more than welcome to try!

To help showcase the Razor in action, this section includes several hypothetical examples of how the Razor could have been used to conceptualise what I consider to be various CVCs. These examples will involve peeling out specific design aspects of pre-existing games in order to create a pencil-sketch vision of something akin to the given target.

It is also worth noting that, while the Razor is just one of the three conceptualisation methodologies captured in this book which have served me well when it comes to high-level concepts, it is the only one that (as we will cover later) must be included in the first page of your pitch document. As such, you are free to either use the Razor upfront, or retroactively create a Razor after arriving at a high-level concept via one of the alternative methodologies. The reason for this is that – the clarity a Razor can offer when it comes to high-level concepts aside – Razors can offer readers an additional degree of confidence in your pitch by showcasing successful video games it is predicated on.

2.5.1.1 Example A

Our first example is *Minecraft*, a CVC if ever there was one, featuring a player versus environment (PvE) sandbox-style survival game wherein players use virtual blocks to build and explore procedurally generated 3D worlds through a first-person camera, primarily focusing on player-driven goals, discovery and player creativity to build just about anything they can imagine.

A potential Razor for *Minecraft* at a pitch level could look something like Table 2.2.

Table 2.2 Razor Example – *Minecraft*

Razor Target: Minecraft		
Spelunky	*Elder Scrolls*	*Lego*™
Proc-gen environments	**Open-world adventure**	**Make anything**
~	~	~
Cave-diving	**First-person camera**	**Blocks that *click* together**
~		
Orthogonal enemies	~	~
	Melee combat	**Creativity-focused**

There are, of course, a lot of important design decisions between this hypothetical version of *Minecraft* and the playable version, be it how those "building blocks" actually work, what weapons should exist or how combat should feel – much of which can be explored and elaborated on later in the pitch document.

You may have also noticed that I used *LEGO™* in the Razor which I included in order to highlight a very important point when it comes to hybridisation: that you are by no means restricted to combining aspects from just video games. By doing so, we in turn restrict the creative possibilities of the Razors we create! It would be (to stick with the chef analogy just a bit longer) a bit like limiting ourselves to a specific food group in our recipes. This point brings us on rather neatly to our second example!

2.5.1.2 Example B

Psyonix's *Rocket League* (whose ingenious Razor I will forever be envious of) essentially combines football and racing, offering a third-person player versus player (PvP) experience wherein players control rocket-powered cars in an attempt to score goals by knocking a ball into the opposing team's net.

Based on this synopsis and my previous point regarding the use of *LEGO™* – a non-video game reference – in our first example of the Razor, this next example in Table 2.3 shouldn't come as much of a surprise!

One of the Razor's key benefits in comparison to the other two methodologies, as this example will hopefully illustrate when you come to reading more about them, is its ability to provide a relatively clear vision of your high-level concept by covering several of the aforementioned

Table 2.3 Razor Example – *Rocket League*

Remote-Controlled Cars	Football
Non-realistic/approachable driving	**Team-based PvP gameplay**
~	~
~	**Goals = winning**
Trick moves	~
~	**Professional sport theming**
Highly responsive control	

Prime Aspects in one concise format. In the case of *Rocket League's* hypothetical Razor, I would like to think that the Razor alone creates a fairly immediate picture of the overall experience that not only feels fun despite existing on nothing but paper, but quickly conveys several of said aspects from camera perspective to game-feel and win/loss conditions.

This example also touches upon a pattern I have often experienced when it comes to particularly strong Razors, wherein combining ingredients of similar appeal to the given intended target audience (a.k.a. customer) can prove highly beneficial to a high-level concept. In other words: if you plan on cooking for someone who you know enjoys a particular cuisine, it probably isn't wise to attempt combining different cuisines, rather than simply trying to give them what they want! After all, what good is a professional chef who only ever cooks for themselves, or worse still ignores the preferences of their clientele?

> Design is not Art. Design is doing something for people to make it fit their needs.
>
> –Don Norman[13]

Where *Rocket League's* Razor is concerned, bearing this analogy and Don Norman's insight in mind, one could argue that it is composed of references belonging to the same "cuisine". It is fairly likely football enthusiasts would consider remote-controlled cars compelling as opposed to something like (for example) fashion makeovers. This is not to say that there would be anything wrong with a football/fashion makeover Razor, that such a Razor couldn't work or that no one would play the resulting video game. But as I have previously stressed: the purpose of this book's process is to land on a relatively safe bet when it comes to your video game pitch achieving CVC status.

Speaking of which . . .

2.5.1.3 Example C

In this example, I would like to introduce additional utility to the Razor wherein it can be used to help define and communicate specific areas of your video game, as opposed to the comparatively more blended styles of Razor we have covered so far.

Take a look at the example in Table 2.4 and note the call-outs beneath each of the references' titles.

Table 2.4 Razor Example – *Deathloop*

Dishonoured (Core Gameplay)	Outer Wilds (Dynamic)	Dead Cells (Meta)
First-person shooter action ~ *Magical* **abilities and non-linear level design that allow for unique solutions**	**A set time-loop**	**Roguelite progression (i.e. player death = player power increase)** ~ **Biome-specific boss fights**

As you can see, rather than each reference calling out an assortment of elements that relate to various Prime Aspects, each of the Razor's references includes the terms such as 'Core Gameplay, 'Dynamic' and 'Meta' clearly indicating the specific areas of the video game they relate to.

I should also point out that, while this example includes reference call-outs that are fairly long in comparison to the call-outs in the other examples provided, this is purely because they were written as examples only. I would highly advise trying to keep your own call-outs concise and clear (preferably no longer than three to four words per call-out) to ensure your Razor doesn't require you having to sacrifice important word-count real estate and fits on your first page – which we will be covering later in this book.

2.5.2 The Twist

Our second methodology is a little something I like to call the Twist which, despite sounding like an antiquated dance move, is in fact a particularly effective way of generating high-level concepts which is somewhat less reliant on familiarity with existing video games than the Razor – but it certainly won't hurt to utilise said familiarity if you have it.

Rather than combining multiple design aspects from varying references (as we did with the Razor) the Twist involves drastically changing just one fundamental area of an existing CVC's design, or rather, putting a "twist" on it. Some examples of this could be:

- Changing the camera perspective (e.g. first-person instead of third-person)
- Changing the player count (e.g. multiplayer instead of single player)
- Changing the player dynamic (e.g. PvP instead of PvE)
- Changing the skill barrier (e.g. pick-up-and-play instead of hardcore)
- Changing the tone (e.g. broad audience instead of mature)

In short, the goal of the Twist is to explore how a single aspect of a pre-existing reference could be altered to offer a distinct-yet-familiar experience and observe what possibilities such a change could lead to.

As with the Razor, the examples we will be covering are by no means a suggestion that they were created this way, nor are they an attempt to diminish all of the important design and/or artistic decisions that make them the successful designs they are! Their only purpose is to try and convey how the Twist could theoretically be used to identify that all-important first step towards their CVC: a pencil sketch (in the design sense of the phrase) of what could be with further work and consideration.

This particular conceptualisation methodology just so happens to be my personal favourite and one I would highly recommend trying on for size. Considering its popularity – indicated by its undeniable commercial success – what might *Fall Guys: Ultimate Knock-out* for a more mature and hardcore player look like? How could *Dark Souls* for a younger audience play out? What if *Animal Crossing* included combat? Maybe one of you will take the time to explore answers to these questions for me!

2.5.2.1 Example A

If one were to take Nintendo's hugely popular and highly successful *Super Mario 64* – which I would argue was very much a CVC of its time – and apply a modern-day battle royale twist to the experience, one could argue that such a high-level concept could potentially land somewhere in the ballpark of Mediatonic's *Fall Guys: Ultimate Knock-out*: a platformer-orientated experience that retains the approachable tone and gameplay of the original reference while producing an entirely unique experience by twisting its player-count.

As mentioned earlier, this twist alone by no means leads straight to the given example. Simply "adding more players" to something like *Super Mario 64* would only produce a *Mario* experience wherein several players are (no doubt chaotically) jumping around levels together. That being said, I cannot help but wonder how long it would take in this imaginary scenario until they started organically racing each other to reach the end of the level, or flinging themselves at each other in a bid to knock each other off platforms. . . . It does however, in my opinion at least, take a step in the right direction – wherein more steps may be taken down that road by asking additional design-related questions. This process, as illustrated in Figure 2.7, can be a little bit like having a conversation with yourself – however crazy that admittedly sounds . . .

If you are lucky enough to have a relative, friend, partner, colleague or rubber duck[14] that would be willing to have such a conversation with you, this back-and-forth process is a lot more fun! Ask as many questions as you can that apply to the problem you are attempting to solve, regardless of how silly you think they may sound or forward-looking they may seem. You would be surprised how beneficial it can be to write such questions out and identify what you know and, more importantly, what you don't.

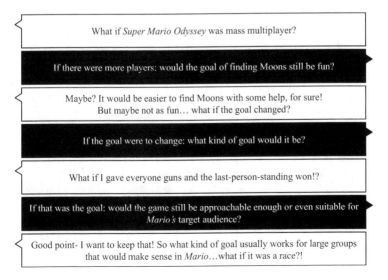

Figure 2.7 The Twist – a conversation with oneself.

2.5.2.2 Example B

Our next example involves Nintendo's time-honoured CVC *Super Smash Bros* – which I would argue twisted the approachability and resulting target audience of preceding fighter-based video games.

Prior to its initial release in 1999,[15] video games belonging to the fighter genre (many of which are CVCs in their own right) typically featured design decisions that tailor them for comparatively hardcore players, given their relatively mature visuals and reliance on memory when it comes to keeping track of numerous button combos. For instance, *Mortal Kombat 11's* Johnny Cage character, between his fatalities, brutalities, basic and special moves boasts (by my own personal count) a whopping 63 attacks that each require specific input sequences.[16]

Conversely, *Super Smash Bros. Ultimate's* very own Mario offers players (again – by my own personal count) a total of 18 different attacks.[17] I would argue that such a design choice could be arrived at through an initial twist of the typical target audience of fighter-style video games: 'if *Mortal Kombat's* target audience was broadened in order to provide more players with access to the genre – what would it take to make that happen?'

2.5.2.3 Example C

Another hypothetical example of the Twist in action might include Santa Monica Studios' critically acclaimed *God of War* – another personal favourite![18] The first era of the franchise, beginning with an initial and hugely successful release in 2005,[19] was a top-down experience focusing on hack'n'slash action.

One could argue that by applying a *Batman: Arkham Asylum*-style over-the-shoulder twist to the original *God Of War's* camera and accompanying higher fidelity visuals, the resulting high-level concept could lead to *God Of War's* equally renowned 2018[20] second era – maintaining the IP's hack'n'slash roots while facilitating a more immersive experience in terms of both combat (by placing players more "in the fight") and narrative (by allowing players to see the facial expressions of the cast).

Just as *Smash Bros'* Twist didn't simply drop Nintendo characters into a *Mortal Kombat*-style experience with lower input complexity, it is important to note that I am not suggesting *God of War 2018* simply slapped Kratos into *Batman: Arkham Asylum*, especially as this subtle distinction lies at the heart of the Twist's effectiveness. Despite applying a significant twist to its gameplay camera, *God of War 2018* retained aspects of the original *God of War's* design formula (be it the brutality of its combat or emphasis on weapon-switching) that were vital to its unique identity, rather than assimilate its hypothetical reference entirely to the point of including a counter-attack command and shoving a cowl over Kratos' head. In other words, it clearly didn't try to be like *Batman: Arkham Asylum*, but it may have seen the benefits such a camera had and how those benefits could not only augment the *God of War* experience but also help it appeal to a target audience who would likely resonate well with it.

Try to remember that the whole point of the Twist is to change one (and only one) fundamental aspect of an existing reference and observe what design questions organically arise when said reference is passed through that lens. In the case of *God of War 2018*, such questions could have been how its combat should work (and feel) through such a camera, how enemy designs would be affected or how its storytelling could take advantage of such a perspective.

2.5.2.4 Example D

While reviewing the various examples I have offered during my umpteenth and increasingly self-critical proof-reading as my deadline grew steadily closer, I realised that between titles like *Rocket League* and *Deathloop*, all of my examples revolve around video games of relatively large scope.

I would therefore like to offer you an additional bonus example of how the Twist could be used to arrive at something comparatively smaller but by no means less successful, which in this case, is Steve Howse's 2016 unprecedented success *Slither.io*.[21] Considering their similarities, such as camera perspective, in-game avatar and player objective, one could argue that *Slither.io* twisted the original *Snake* (1976) – later popularised by a re-release on Nokia mobiles in the 1990s[22] – by (likeable to Example A) modifying the original reference's player count.

As with our other examples, while there are important and undeniable design differences between these two video games, be it the more approachable art style or the ability to cross over yourself in *Slither.io*, simply twisting *Snake's* player count and dynamic (i.e. introducing a battle royale element) produces a high-level concept that is quite close to the final outcome. As highlighted by *TheGamer*'s Eric Switzer in his 2019 article 'Where Slither.io Came From And Why It's So Popular':

> The one thing *Slither.io* [had] that *Agar.io* [did] not . . . is a connection to that classic arcade game and the first mobile game all of us ever played, *Snake*.
>
> – Eric Switzer[23]

This astute call-out relates to what we touched on at the start of this section: that Twists can be particularly effective because, on a fundamental level, they can produce distinct-yet-familiar experiences that can greatly benefit from said familiarity.

2.5.3 Verbification

If you are entirely unfamiliar with the term Verbification or what it means, that's probably because it is a Frankensteinian term I unashamedly smashed together one day which (if you hadn't guessed already) is a fusion of the words 'verb' and 'gamification'.

This third short-and-sweet conceptualisation methodology focuses on the main ability or core activity of your high-level concept. Grand visions and stellar storytelling are all very well and good, but a truly compelling core mechanic can be timeless, be it slotting tetriminos together or playing with a pair of portals.

The Verbification process is fairly simple and involves simply attaching an '-ing' to the end of a word to create a verb that is yet to be gamified and exploring its possibilities – some examples of which might include:

- Parkour [ing] → *Mirror's Edge*
- Obstacle-course [ing] → *Fall Guys: Ultimate Knock-out*
- Jump [ing] → *Mario*
- Run [ing] → *Sonic*
- Portal [ing] → *Portal*
- Eat [ing] → *Pac-Man*

Consider the fact that many modern games are iterations of an early ancestor (more often than not a CVC) that first thought to gamify a particular verb. For example, did you know that *Maze Wars*, originally developed in 1973, was the first game to feature first-person shooting?[24] While it may not have reached the heights of those that came after it, it nevertheless heralded the early beginnings of an entire genre, which isn't too bad for a group of high school students.

This methodology can, admittedly, feel a bit like searching for a needle in the metaphorical haystack. You will find that many (and what may feel like all) of your Verbification attempts have already been done before – and at some point I imagine that may indeed be the case. While one of Verbification's key benefits is the lesser reliance it has on familiarity with existing references – even more-so than the Twist – that is also undoubtedly one of its key drawbacks. But considering some of the aforementioned examples, some of which are fairly recent, it may be the case that there's still more than a few very valuable make-shift verbs left.

Furthermore, in my experience, Verbifications typically produce mechanics-focused high-level concepts that initially appear overly simplistic. Never forget that simple ideas can be the most powerful! If an idea is only as powerful as the number of people who buy into it, I have often found that simple ideas often work well because they are easy to understand and buy into – and understanding typically facilitates fun.

2.6 CLONING VERSUS REFERENCING

Considering the important role of pre-existing references in the majority of the conceptualisation methodologies we have covered, it is important to understand the differences between referencing an inspiration and cloning them.

In the video games industry, the term 'clone' is used to describe video games which are essentially copies of already existing games, but you may be wondering where referencing ends and cloning begins. To my mind this important difference is best reflected by one of my all-time favourite quotes:

> Good artists copy, great artists steal.
>
> – Pablo Picasso[25]

While there is some dispute around whether it was indeed Picasso who originally voiced this notion,[26] to try and break down what he may have meant, a 'good artist' will typically see another artist's work and attempt to essentially reproduce said work – even if that means straight-up copying it. A 'great artist', on the other hand, will typically see another artist's work and attempt to incorporate specific aspects of it into their own in order to create something new – yet similar.

Assuming you prescribe to Picasso's viewpoint, whom I think it is safe to say knew a thing or two about the creative process, I would argue that the key difference between referencing and cloning ultimately comes down to overall similarity. For example, take a look at Figures 2.8 – 2.10 in Table 2.5.

Table 2.5 Cloning Versus Referencing

Original Work	New Work A	New Work B
Figure 2.8 Original work.	*Figure 2.9* New work (A).	*Figure 2.10* New work (B).

If we were to imagine that the 'Original Work' entry was a video game, 'New Work (A)' would be akin to slightly modifying the art style or changing literally nothing else but the platform, retaining pretty much everything else from mechanics and player count to camera perspective and player goals. You may be thinking to yourself: 'wait . . . isn't that exactly what the Twist is all about?' – and understandably so. It is important to remember that, while this may indeed sound like the Twist at first glance (i.e. changing one fundamental aspect of the original reference), the purpose of the Twist is not solely about just changing one aspect of the original reference's design – but to explore what other changes such a change could incur to its overall design. Conversely, while 'New Work (B)' bears similarities to 'Original Work' and has certainly incorporated aspects of it, it also includes clear differences. This is not to falsely suggest that clones – as I have defined them in this book at least – have never been or can never be CVCs. My only aim here is to illustrate in as simple terms as possible what I would argue the difference is between referencing and cloning, considering how central referencing is to the majority of the conceptualisation methodologies covered.

What makes the methodologies we have covered so effective in my experience is that they are predicated on precisely what I believe Picasso considered great artists do – selectively referencing rather than wholesale copying – which can offer you several important advantages when properly understood and utilised.

From a designer standpoint, you can see how something feels or works immediately, without having to develop it yourself. For instance, if you were designing for a specific audience and know of an existing reference whose controls were well received by that same audience, it is far cheaper and quicker to simply try out that reference yourself and validate the direction rather than spending time and resources to find out. Work smart – not hard!

From a pitch and player standpoint, it can also help others quickly understand what your concept might be like to play, especially if they are particularly familiar with the references involved. To offer an example, if your pitch revolved around a battle royale-style version of Atari engineer Allan Alcorn's *Pong*,[27] it would be much easier for someone to understand 'it's like *Pong* – but with battle royale multiplayer' rather than trying to explain *Pong* from scratch. In short, the ability for others to understand your video game (pitch or otherwise) in positive and relatable terms, quickly and easily, should never be underestimated – allowing them to quickly determine if it is a game they might enjoy playing, know what is to be expected of them and better understand how to play said game from the get-go.

You may have even experienced this yourself: it is usually much easier to play a game you are already somewhat familiar with, potentially because you recognise aspects of it from other games or life experiences, than to learn how an entirely new game works. Nothing helps players understand the rules of a game better than getting to play it themselves since, to my mind, understanding is often a major prerequisite of fun – have you ever had fun doing something you simply did not or could not understand and did not believe you ever possibly would? This isn't to say that the process of understanding something new isn't fun – far from it! If anything I would argue that the joy of play comes from precisely that: the slow and steady formation of understanding something new. But if ever that understanding fails to materialise, I would be willing to bet that most of the time, fun will also fail to materialise!

This is where our methodologies really shine, in that they allow us to capitalise on pre-existing mental models, which is the way we, as humans, simplify complexity.[28] However hard some of us may try, we are unable to keep all the details of the world in our brains, so we use mental models to simplify the complex into understandable and recallable chunks – including the rules or mechanics of a video game. One of my favourite examples is WeirdBeard's ingenious *Tricky Towers*.

Just by looking at it (go ahead and give it a quick Google – I'll wait) I suspect that many of you will quickly derive how this game works because you are already familiar with *Tetris*. This is the power of utilising mental models and taking inspiration from pre-existing references: the power to communicate the premise and mechanics of a game you may have never even seen before which, again, not only allows players to pick up and play quicker but also better allows them to determine if the game looks like something they would be interested in playing – potentially converting a prospective player into a new user.

Another practical example of this from my very own career involves the design of a game mode called *Dice World Race* in Scopely's casual mobile game *Yahtzee With Buddies*. The objective of this feature was to play games of *Yahtzee* to earn "steps" which moved players around the track – with players who finished in top tier positions winning the best rewards. However, while designing the feature, playtests soon identified an issue wherein players who didn't play as frequently as others could quickly fall far behind in the race, making it impossible to catch up which in turn eroded engagement and retention. To combat this challenge, one of the spaces on the board was converted into a mystery card space which, when landed on, would award players with a random amount of bonus steps – offering stragglers the opportunity to (with a little luck) get back in the race! This mechanic was not plucked out of thin air, but instead inspired by a *Bullet Bill* power-up reference in *Mario Kart*, which hopefully underlines the power of mental models in game design and in turn why referencing can be such a beneficial process for you, your reader and players alike.

While this topic might feel like something of a tangent, it is important to be aware of mental models and their potential benefits to your pitch when writing one, particularly in the context of referencing versus cloning – '*Pong* – but battle royale' being the former and '*Pong* – but blue' arguably being the latter.

2.7 WORKSHOP TASK

2.7.1 Chapter Highlights

- Video game conceptualisation can determine the success potential of a video game long before development even begins.

- Think of the conceptualisation phase of video game development like the foundation of a building – its shape, size and strength will determine everything else that follows.
- CVCs are a calibre of pitch capable of leading to immensely successful video games – be it critically or commercially – that effectively elaborate on and communicate a *Spark*. The blueprint of a video game!
- Sparks are the core of a pitch – and potential CVC – comprising two key elements: design restrictions and a high-level concept.
- Designing by restriction is akin to identifying what paints and canvas size you are working with before you begin painting – you can't start creating until you know what your limitations are. Rather than impede your creativity, this will often lead to unexpected discoveries through necessity.

  - The most important of said design restrictions is opportunity: try to find a substantial and currently unmet need in the marketplace that could capitalise on an existing gaming trend – be it a genre or mechanic.

- Your high-level concept should offer an overview of your video game's experience that doesn't get hung up on the details of exactly how it would work in practice (e.g. procedurally generated world vs. an in-depth breakdown of how procedural generation works).

  - Creating an effective high-level concept can be a bit like cooking in the sense that knowledge of ingredients and their compatibility goes a long way when prepping a potential recipe.

- I have found the three conceptualisation methodologies outlined (the Razor; the Twist; Verbification) to be highly effective when it comes to producing high-level concepts – try each of them to see which works best for you.

  - The Razor can offer a particularly clear vision of a high-level concept but its effectiveness can be influenced by reference familiarity and knowledge. The more ingredients you taste the greater your creative options become.
  - The Twist can offer particularly strong high-level concepts given its capacity for creating distinct-yet-familiar results by altering one fundamental aspect of a high value reference before exploring how that change would impact the overall design.

- Verbification can offer a conceptualisation methodology that is considerably less reliant on any pre-existing knowledge around video games and their design by simply trying to gamify either actual verbs or verbified words. This process can prove instrumental in identifying entirely new gameplay experiences – be it competing in an obstacle course-inspired game show or parkouring across a cityscape.

- While the majority of the conceptualisation methodologies covered in this book utilise existing references it is important to understand the difference between referencing and cloning. The goal of these methodologies is not to copy, but to create something distinct-yet-familiar, ensuring that your pitch will not only resonate with the intended target audience but help others (including said audience) quickly and easily understand the experience on offer and instantly know whether it's of interest to them.

2.7.2 Reader Assignment

1. Outline your design restrictions – including:

   a. Opportunity
   b. Intended Target Audience
   c. Scope
   d. Resources
   e. Platform

2. Use one of the conceptualisation methodologies (the Razor; the Twist; Verbification) to come up with a high-level concept that meets the requirements of your aforementioned design restrictions.

NOTES

1. www.open.ac.uk/blogs/design/necessity-is-the-mother-of-invention
2. https://surveypal.fi/en/2016/steve-jobs-said-it-best-start-with-the-customer-experience/
3. www.wired.co.uk/article/werewolf
4. nintendolife.com/news/2012/03/the_mystery_of_the_super_mario_bros_us_release_date
5. www.smithsonianmag.com/science-nature/math-card-game-spot-it-180970873/
6. toynews-online.biz/2019/01/17/dobble-named-uks-biggest-selling-card-game-as-one-millionth-unit-sold/

7. webtribunal.net/blog/destiny-2-player-count/#gref

8. ign.com/articles/2013/12/07/destiny-release-date-announced

9. wired.com/2007/10/its-official-bu/

10. eurogamer.net/microsoft-held-talks-to-buy-bungie-report

11. www.youtube.com/watch?v=v28OYL4xikk&t=66s&ab_channel=IGN

12. https://web.archive.org/web/20130610034155/http://ps3.mmgn.com/News/the-last-of-us-inspired-by-ico-re4

13. www.interaction-design.org/master-classes/exclusive-design-for-a-better-world-a-discussion-with-don-norman

14. Andrew Hunt and David Thomas, The Pragmatic Programmer

15. www.ign.com/games/super-smash-bros

16. www.ign.com/wikis/mortal-kombat-11/Johnny_Cage

17. www.eventhubs.com/moves/ssb4/mario/

18. My saying this has absolutely nothing to do with any minor man-crush on Cory Barlog . . . nothing whatsoever . . .

19. www.playstation.com/en-gb/god-of-war/

20. www.playstation.com/en-gb/god-of-war/

21. www.thegamer.com/slitherio-history-success-guide-strategy/

22. www.itsnicethat.com/features/taneli-armanto-the-history-of-snake-design-legacies-230221

23. www.thegamer.com/slitherio-history-success-guide-strategy/

24. https://screenrant.com/doom-quake-wolfenstein-fps-first-person-shooter/

25. www.creativethinkinghub.com/creative-thinking-and-stealing-like-an-artist/

26. www.dklevine.com/papers/b_l_review.pdf

27. www.gamedeveloper.com/business/the-history-of-i-pong-i-avoid-missing-game-to-start-industry

28. https://fs.blog/mental-models/

Chapter 3

Validation

3.1 CHAPTER INTRODUCTION

Conceptualising new ideas for potential pitches is one thing, but how do we determine if our Spark has what it takes to become a CVC were it to be fully developed, especially at such an early point in a video game's lifespan when it only exists on paper?

While spending time and resources on developing a prototype or possibly even waiting until some form of early access to find out is certainly an option, as I have previously mentioned, this option is rarely quick – or cheap!

Between a (quite literal) lifetime fascination with playing industry-defining video games spanning from the 1980s to present day and ten years of firsthand industry experience, the majority of which has been spent honing this book's vision-crafting process through writing (again – quite literally) countless pitches for various companies interested in launching the next big hit, it is my belief that the majority of CVCs possess several similar characteristics regardless of their genre or era. As such, this chapter is dedicated to listing out and explaining several questions to ask of your Spark based on these shared qualities in order to validate its CVC probability, just as developers typically create prototypes to validate their theories (see Figure 3.1).

It should come as little surprise that the conceptual tool for this validation assumes the form of something perfectly suited for bottling lighting . . .

DOI: 10.1201/9781003269632-3

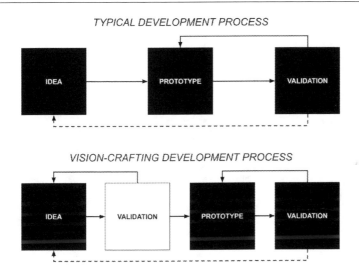

Figure 3.1 Vision-crafting versus typical development.

3.2 THE LIGHTNING ROD

The Lightning Rod (see Figure 3.2) is the visual representation of the aforementioned questions to ask of your concept before proceeding to Chapter 4 and either expanding upon or articulating it on paper – a means of evaluating whether your infant pitch has the potential to become a CVC and is a foundation worth building on top of.

Like any system, it is far from foolproof, nor does it 100% guarantee your pitch will become a CVC. Just because the ground floor is solid it doesn't automatically mean that the rest of the building is completely unimportant. It only means that it has a solid foundation which has set it on the right course – with both marketing and execution playing important roles when it comes to any video game achieving CVC-level status. That being said, the questions listed throughout the following pages are my definitive go-tos which have served me extremely well to date when it comes to pitching CVCs and it is my sincere hope that they serve you too. At best, the Lightning Rod will guide you towards a CVC; at worst, it should help you design a better game. Something of a win-win situation by all accounts!

Each of these key questions could be equated to "rungs" on a light-ning rod – hence the analogy – which your Spark must pass through

Figure 3.2 The Lightning Rod.

in order for it to reach the poorly illustrated bottle at the bottom and give us (you guessed it) bottled lightning. If a Spark fails to satisfy a particular rung – don't panic! This doesn't necessarily mean that your Spark is not CVC-worthy or that you should start again from Chapter 1, but the more rungs a Spark successfully passes through, the better.

3.2.1 Rung #1: Does Your High-Level Concept Meet Your Design Restrictions?

If you took the time to truly understand and identify your design restrictions earlier in the process, odds are that your Spark is already infused and informed by this information and should pass through this rung with flying colours!

Nevertheless, it is good practice to reevaluate your high-level concept and ensure that it does indeed still satisfy the design restrictions you originally outlined for yourself, be it the scope of the experience, whether that core experience is suitable for the intended target audience's preferences and needs and (perhaps most importantly) if there is an opportunity for it to succeed. It is understandably easy to get carried away or swept up in excitement during such a freeform creative process as conceptualisation, where anything is possible until reality comes crashing in and you realise you have gotten lost along the way, or tried to bite off far more than you could possibly chew. So go through the list of restrictions you initially set yourself, one by one, and ensure your pitch still aligns with all of them.

3.2.2 Rung #2: Does It Do Anything First or Best?

3.2.2.1 Doing It First

Consider video games such as *Tetris* or *Portal*: video games that introduced a player-controlled mechanic or specific experience before any other video game.

To clarify, the term 'mechanic' essentially refers to an ability the player can perform in-game, be it creating a pair of interconnected portals or rotating bricks in order to slot them together and create rows that clear themselves when solidified.

Video games that coin specific mechanics or experiences first can prove to be incredibly powerful, namely because mechanics are the distinguishing hallmarks of the video game medium which, unlike any other, bastions interactivity at its core (see Table 3.1).

As such, a truly unique mechanic or experience can often (but not always – as we are about to touch on) be tantamount to gold-dust, assuming said mechanic or experience is presented in a fashion capable of attracting the audience it is intended for! Which neatly brings us the second half of this particular rung . . .

Table 3.1 Doing It First – Examples

CVC (A–Z)	What They Did First
Minecraft	Turning LEGO™ bricks into a video game
Portal	Using portals to solve puzzles
Shin Megami Tensei	Catching monsters to use in battle

3.2.2.2 Doing It Best

I fully appreciate that the term 'best' is, at first glance, incredibly subjective and vague, so allow me to try and define what this word means in the context of this chapter.

Simply put, I define 'best' in the context of video game design as that which:

1. Identifies and addresses design issues with competitors that make meaningful or valuable improvements on them for the given intended target audience, and/or;
2. Offers an alternate execution of the competitor that is more conducive with the audience said competitor typically attracts

Regarding point 1: addressing these *design issues* could include anything from juicier gameplay – such as visual and/or auditory inputs that help make the game feel more satisfying – to enhanced visuals, improved UX (User Experience), better writing or more player-considerate mechanics that improve upon their typical designs. Think of it like creating Haiwaiian pizzas for Haiwaiian pizza-loving customers that offer significantly more pineapple than the existing Haiwaiian pizzerias do – a metaphor I am fully aware risks at least half of you disposing of this book immediately! To put it in other words: try to understand what players of an already popular experience want more (or less) of and factor that into your pitch.

As for point 2, here's a quick example. It is often believed that Nintendo's arcade classic *Donkey Kong*, released in 1981, was the first video game to feature the jump mechanic.[1] As it so happens, this mechanic first appeared six years prior to *Donkey Kong* in Atari's arcade title, *Steeplechase*, whose high-level concept clearly differed dramatically from *Donkey Kong's* and focused on the core fantasy of horse racing – tasking players with jumping over obstacles to successfully reach the finish line first.[2] Similarly to *Donkey Kong*, jumps were the same height and length, regardless of how long players pressed the jump button. So the question is: why did *Steeplechase* fail to achieve the level of success *Donkey Kong* accomplished despite featuring the same primary mechanic?[3]

It could be attributed to a variety of factors, such as simply being in the right place at the right time, smarter marketing or anything else you might wish to call out and maybe that's all entirely true! But I would argue that one of the main reasons *Donkey Kong* reached the lofty heights of CVC status over *Steeplechase* is that it satisfied this very rung of our Lightning Rod: by utilising the mechanic *best* which – in this case and to say the least – involved offering more decision-making around when to jump, more control regarding jump direction and presenting it in a wrapper that resonated better with audiences attracted to mastering the jump.

Speaking of mastery . . .

3.2.3 Rung #3: Does It Offer Room for Player Improvement?

Why do you think tetrominoes begin to fall faster and faster in *Tetris* the longer you play? Or why levels in *Mario* get progressively harder over time?

The short answer is because, as a player plays your video game, they will naturally improve at it. This is the case for anything we spend our time on – be it a video game or sweet back-flips – until we eventually (assuming we continue to engage with the activity) master it. The trouble is, once we *master* something, we can often find that it quickly becomes repetitive – or even boring.

> Mastery requires practice. But the more you practice something, the more boring and routine it becomes. . . . We get bored with habits because they stop delighting us. The outcome becomes expected . . . our habits become ordinary [and] we start derailing our progress to seek novelty.
>
> – James Clear[4]

As a result, well-designed video games – and CVCs in particular – typically provide players with a long runway to achieving mastery over time, starting them off easy (in relation to the audience it is intended for) and gradually increasing the level of mastery required over time in order to ensure that players keep playing and enjoy themselves – CVCs such as *Candy Crush Saga* with its 12,500 levels worth of runway being a prime example.[5] It truly is all about the journey – not the final level!

Some additional examples have been listed in Table 3.2 to further illustrate the concept.

It is worth noting that, as illustrated in Figures 3.3 to 3.4 of Table 3.3, particularly well-designed games don't do this in a purely linear fashion, but instead offer the player moments of reprieve along the way, wherein the mastery needed is dropped to some degree or another.

There is, unfortunately, one important challenge to consider with the offer of mastery over time: content. Be it new levels, quests, abilities, enemies and anything in between, all of this content could be equated to individual bricks for your "mastery runway" – which the

Table 3.2 Examples of Player Improvement *Runways* in Existing CVCs

CVC (A–Z)	Key Player Improvement Runway
Mario	The player . . . masters the timing and weight of Mario's jump
Minecraft	The player . . . masters knowledge of the world and its various entities
Overwatch	The player . . . masters first-person shooting and character skills
Pokemon	The player . . . masters Pokemon strengths and weaknesses
Rocket League	The player . . . masters control of their rocket-powered car or how the ball behaves when struck

Table 3.3 Linear Versus Non-linear Mastery

Linear Mastery	Non-linear Mastery

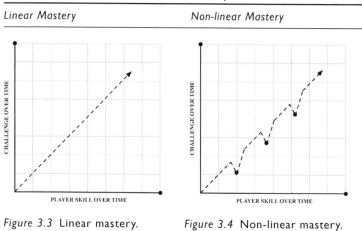

Figure 3.3 Linear mastery.   *Figure 3.4* Non-linear mastery.

player will rarely reverse along and costs both time and money to create and further extend the runway. This disinterest in reversing typically arises, in my opinion, from the fact that almost all games (digital or not) are ultimately puzzles of varying complexity or style. They are something for the participant to figure out and solve in some form or other in exchange for the same pleasant outcomes: a sense of achievement from greater mastery, cognitive flow[6] and a well-earned injection of dopamine.[7] The concept of "fun" or "play" is essentially the result of a brain being presented with a problem it enjoys and is capable of solving, whether it is figuring out what shapes go in which holes, when to jump or where to shoot. However, as with any puzzle, they are a lot less fun after being solved – I doubt you have ever wanted to complete the same crossword more than once.

It is for this reason that PvE CVCs can be much greater in scope than PvP CVCs: because of all the unique puzzles (i.e. content) they can require just to keep players engaged and lengthen that runway. The only thing that can compete against the ultimate problem solver is another problem solver of equal capability: another player. The unstoppable force to your immovable object! PvP video games essentially turn players into "runway bricks" for each other, simply because playing against a human opponent can provide a near never-ending puzzle. While an AI-controlled enemy's attacks and movements can be learned, mastered and better predicted over time, an opposing player is infinitely more dynamic and unpredictable, creating endless permutations of experience wherein no two encounters are ever quite the same. A certain level may only be played once in a PvE game, but used countless times in a PvP game, where it serves as an arena rather than a singular experience.

This is not to say that the only means of achieving a longer runway more efficiently is dependent on the inclusion of multiplayer, especially when PvP video games most definitely have costs and complications of their own. Developers have come up with all manner of smart design solutions to encourage content recycling in PvE video games, be it high scores, difficulty settings, different endings depending on the choices made throughout the game, collectibles or procedurally generated environments to name a select few – not to mention the entire roguelike genre!

But considering the monumental success of specifically PvP multiplayer CVCs such as *Fortnite*, *League of Legends* and *Mario Kart*, it is a noteworthy pattern to be aware of.

3.2.4 Rung #4: Does the Puzzle Match the Player?

As mentioned earlier, I would argue that every video game is ultimately just another puzzle for someone to solve, recreating an age-old relationship between puzzle-creator and puzzle-solver. As designers (i.e. the puzzle creators) it is our responsibility to ensure that the puzzles we produce attract the puzzle-solvers it is intended for and, more importantly, that they can eventually be cracked (because why would anyone want to spend time on a puzzle that has literally no solution?) without simply giving the solution away, but instead allow the puzzle solver to figure it out for themselves – potentially teaching them how to do so over time and offering positive feedback for their efforts along the way.

This applies to video games that seemingly have no relationship whatsoever with what you may consider puzzle solving to be. Let's use iD Software's timeless 1993 first-person shooter *DOOM* as an example – another CVC if ever there was one! For anyone unfamiliar with *DOOM*, players are tasked with fighting through a series of non-linear levels in search of the exit, all of which are strewn with up to seven distinct enemy designs hellbent on tearing you to pieces.

Thankfully *DOOM* arms players with an equally distinct variety of firearms with which to overcome the demonic hordes that stand in their way – and this is where the puzzle solving begins. As quoted by *GMTK's* Mark Brown (big fan) in his superb episode 'What Can We Learn From *DOOM*':

> The reason *DOOM* works so well is because each enemy represents a distinct, consistent, and discernable behaviour that can be learned.
>
> – Matthias Worch[8]

To further quote said *GMTK* episode:

> This is what Deux Ex designer Harvey Smith (game designer at Arkane Studios) calls 'orthogonal unit differentiation', which basically means that the [different enemies] have completely unique attributes, rather than just being more or less powerful versions of each other . . . what this means, according to Smith, is that you start 'playing intentionally', and making meaningful, tactical decisions – not just randomly reacting to what's going on.
>
> – Mark Brown[9]

As a result, one could argue that every combat encounter in *DOOM* is, essentially, unique and distinct puzzles (comprising the enemies, environment or player tools they utilise) for the player to solve, featuring a multitude of questions the player must simultaneously answer on-the-fly – including:

- 'Which enemy should I prioritise?'
- 'Where should I move to in order to avoid attacks?'

- 'Where will that enemy move to?'
- 'Which weapon is best suited for dealing with the next enemy?'
- 'How could I overcome this challenge in the most efficient way possible?'

If the combat encounters in *DOOM* were a crossword, consider its enemies to be the clues and the weapons to be the pen with which to write answers, ultimately culminating in a sizable series of puzzles for the player to solve. Somewhat intense, sure, but puzzles nonetheless! However, considering the volume/rate of questions and motor skills its puzzles require, the kind of puzzles *DOOM* presents its players with are by no means suitable for everyone and anyone – young children being an obvious example. It is important to note that the latter would be the case regardless of *DOOM*'s suitability for children on a thematic level: if its demons were swapped out for teddy bears and its firearms for magic spells, but the mechanics and pacing remained, I still highly doubt such an experience would be feasible for a 6-year-old!

Therefore, considering the fact that not every puzzle is suitable for every audience, the purpose of this rung is to ensure not only that your pitch will be capable of attracting the puzzle-solvers it is intended for, but also that the puzzles it features will be suitable for them. In *DOOM*'s case, its mature and oh-so-satisfyingly gory wrapper arguably attracted the kind of puzzle-solver perfectly suited for the intense, fast-paced, hand/eye-coordination style of puzzle it offers – a vein of puzzle-solver that were vast enough in number to create CVC-level results. In short, different types of puzzles require very different skills, which I believe typically comes down to two key factors: dexterity and focus (see Figure 3.5). The term 'dexterity', in this context, refers to both the number of commands involved (i.e. buttons to press) and how quickly they must be pressed; whereas 'focus' refers to how intensely (on a second-to-second basis) the player must concentrate on the video game in order to avoid failure.

So ask yourself: would the style of puzzle you are creating tap into a large vein of players who would be capable of and willing to solve your puzzle?

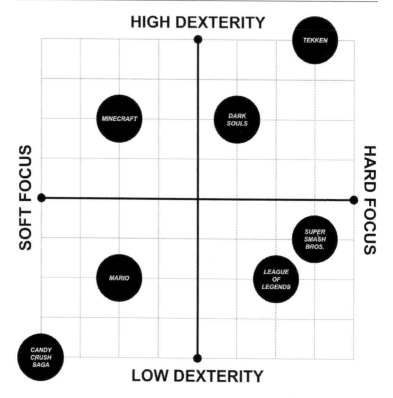

Figure 3.5 Dexterity versus Focus cross-axis.

3.2.5 Rung #5: Does It Exhibit Conduciveness?

As Sadhguru, an Indian yoga guru, once said:

> Children are not your property . . . It's a privilege – another life came through you. You must enjoy it. Do your best to nourish it. What it becomes is not your business. Your business is to . . . create an ambience where it grows well. Like a tree; like a plant. You just create the nourishment that it needs [so that] it grows.
>
> – Sadhguru[10]

I am fairly confident this was the last sort of person you were expecting to see being quoted in a book about creating video game pitches, but nevertheless, this philosophy very much relates to a quality I like to call Conduciveness – which some Sparks will possess a greater or lesser affinity for than others.

Conducive design, as I have coined it, is essentially the process of identifying design choices that naturally and intuitively arise from one another during conceptualisation and development: choices that follow on almost organically from each other while still adhering to and growing from your video game's point of origin – your Spark. One of my favourite examples of what could be considered conducive design is the headshot mechanic, wherein shots that strike the head of an in-game target, while being harder to hit successfully, typically reward the player's precise aim with bonus damage. This mechanic was first introduced by Sega's *Virtua Cop* arcade games before finding its way into other reputable CVCs such as *Resident Evil*[11] and is now a staple of most shooters – such is the power of conducive design! This mechanic can be considered a great example of conducive design in that – as a design choice – it is a natural evolution of its preceding mechanic (i.e. more precise aiming) that not only adheres to but enhances the core fantasy (i.e. being really good at shooting stuff!).

The more opportunities a Spark offers for this organic style of design, the easier you will find it to conceptually develop and instil your pitch with what I refer to as Harmony: a certain quality of video game design wherein the various facets of an experience, from its art style and musical score to its level design or progression, are informed by and related to one another – all originating from (ideally) a conducive design-friendly Spark at its core. For instance, imagine a video game that looked and played exactly like *Mario*, but featured a heavy metal soundtrack instead of its signature melodies as well as the ability to pull out a highly realistic AK-47, capable of gorily gunning down Goombas. As hilarious and entertaining as these changes might sound, my hope is that both of them nevertheless strike you as "disharmonious", given how divorced they are from the rest of the experience and in turn how harmful they would be to the design's harmony. This is not to say people wouldn't play it – but I would be surprised if such a version of *Mario* would achieve the same level of CVC status! Alternatively, imagine a universe wherein *Minecraft* featured high fidelity visuals, twitchy combat and gruesome death scenes. While the Spark would have remained intact, the execution and presentation of said Spark would have placed it in the hands of a very different player-base, rather than allowing it to tap into the vast vein of players it ultimately tapped into through its family-friendly mechanics and aesthetic.

A particularly great example of Harmony is Maddy Makes Games' exceptional pixel-art platformer *Celeste*, which we touched on earlier in this book, wherein players are tasked with jumping their way up an increasingly challenging mountain interspersed with cutscenes between the main character (Celeste) and NPCs which explore her efforts towards personal growth. Considering its critical acclaim – scoring 92% on Metacritic[12] – and its several industry awards, clearly *Celeste* did something right, which I would argue emanates (in part – but a large part) from its exceptional conduciveness, such as its pixel-art visuals complementing precise and responsive platformer gameplay or its capacity to attract retro-orientated audiences willing to engage with its skill level. Not to mention its choice of gameworld location – a mountain – emulating the uphill struggle themes of the story.

When it comes to achieving conducive design, I have often found that narrating an idea out can really help. A hypothetical example of this rubber ducking-inspired[13] process has been included in the following extract, which revolves around how Andrew Shouldice's isometric masterpiece *Tunic* could have arrived at the ingenious use of its relatively restrictive isometric camera with regard to world exploration and discovering secrets, by utilising conducive design to find the optimal solution.

> I want this game to have an isometric camera that recreates the retro experience of its references and encourages gameworld map mastery – because players can't just look out to the horizon . . .
>
> But this top-down ceilingless view would make it too easy for players to spot secret areas and hidden rewards, which I also really want in the game, being equally indicative of that retro-inspired experience . . .
>
> . . . What if the isometric camera could be rotated – requiring players to rotate the camera in the right places to reveal hidden treasures?
>
> . . . But this would detract from the retro experience that the game is intended to evoke, not to mention cause a potentially huge impact to the gameworld's design, whose readability and layout will require a lot of time and resources for even just one camera angle . . .
>
> . . . Well, if my camera doesn't have the option of rotating and hidden secrets are a must-have, what if I used this locked perspective to hide secret tunnels and entrances behind environmental props? This would encourage players to explore every nook and cranny of the gameworld and potentially even result in exciting and unexpected discoveries!!

When we stop a Spark from evolving conducively, either by failing to recognise the opportunities for conducive design, ignoring them or even actively fighting against how it wants to grow in favour of personal preferences, it is typically weakened – resulting in a general sense of disjointedness in the design. But again, you may find that some Sparks lend themselves better to conducive design than others and that some will almost grow by themselves, with little effort on your part. How conducive does your Spark seem to be at this point in time?

3.2.6 Rung #6: Does It Prioritise Gameplay?

Consider some of the biggest CVCs out there – video games whose names are recognised around the world:

- *Fortnite*
- *League of Legends*
- *Mario*
- *Minecraft*
- *Overwatch*
- *Zelda*

I would argue that all of these heavyweight CVCs are primarily mechanics-driven rather than narrative-driven: video games which are highly gameplay orientated with less of a focus on spoon-feeding players a scripted story and instead allowing players to create emergent stories of their own – often with each other!

This is most definitely not to say that these CVCs and their ilk don't have a premise or support rich and fascinating lore – only that the primary incentives to play usually revolve around learning and mastering mechanics.

There are, of course, exceptions to the rule (I'm looking at you *Final Fantasy*) – as is always the case! It may very well be that your pitch's narrative has what it takes to help it achieve CVC status. That being said, I would advise you to remember that story-telling is a beast entirely unto itself, which can seriously damage both a pitch and the resulting video game unless said story is exceptionally well executed.

3.2.7 Rung #7: Does It Recreate the Colosseum Effect?

The video games industry exists in an age where video game streaming is more prolific than ever, providing them with greater outreach to prospective new players who could potentially lift it to CVC status, but also heightening the importance of designs that can draw and hold a large audience.

It is my belief that in order for a pitch to satisfy this particular rung, it must capture the same key qualities of the Colosseum, Rome's famous amphitheatre, which I also believe applies to any form of gamified entertainment that includes rules, players and loss conditions – be it Football, Ping Pong or *Call of Duty*! Instilling your video game's design with these key qualities can be achieved well in advance during the pitching stage – better enabling it to create communities around itself. Considering the fact that the Colosseum was not just one person in the audience, but a whole mass of people experiencing and enjoying the same thing in unison, this huge sense of community where people celebrated or cried together turned an otherwise solo activity into something communal – a powerful force which lies at the heart of this rung. Perhaps the term 'CVC' should have stood for 'Commercially Viable Communities' . . . something to explore in a future book perhaps!

So without further ado – the aforementioned key qualities of this final rung of our Lightning Rod include the following.

3.2.7.1 Suspense

I define the term 'suspense' as the sense of excitement players (or in this case *viewers*) experience around not knowing what will happen next, much like the suspense crowds of the Colosseum would have undoubtedly felt from the uncertainty over who would prevail: gladiator or lion! More specifically, it has been my experience that this suspense typically arises from not only the unknown, but an unknown that could potentially lead to failure for one or multiple parties.

Considering the latter, it shouldn't come as a surprise to learn that the majority of 2022's most streamed video games included multiplayer-focused CVCs,[14] wherein said failure lies in one team eventually being vanquished by the other.

- *League of Legends* (1.77 billion)
- *Valorant* (1.3 billion)
- *Apex Legends* (845.3 million)
- *Counter-Strike: Global Offensive* (768.5 million)
- *Fortnite* (738.5 million)
- *Dota 2* (653.5 million)

As humans, we are tentatively attracted to the unknown on a psychological level, driven by a fundamental motivation to seek knowledge through triggered curiosity[15] – making this key quality particularly powerful. So consider where – if anywhere – and to what degree suspense could be propagated by the video game your Spark would lead to.

3.2.7.2 Variety

Picture a strange universe where the exact same events play out at the mighty Colosseum every single day. The exact same fights. The exact same challenges. The exact same victors and losers. Just as most would-be spectators likely wouldn't want to watch the exact same football game several times over, despite newer audiences being suitably pleased, it is unlikely that such entertainment would retain audiences for very long!

This is why, I would argue, so many existing CVCs offer ways of changing up gameplay: to ensure that there's always something new for audiences to see or experience – and to keep that audience captivated for as long as possible (see Table 3.4).

Table 3.4 Examples of How Variety Is Created in Existing CVCs

CVC Examples (A–Z)	Solutions To Variety
Fall Guys: Ultimate Knock-out	Unique levels; multiplayer
Fortnite	Battle royale; randomised loot; multiplayer
God of War	Distinct boss fights; new enemies; new gear/ abilities
Hearthstone	Card-drawing; ever-expanding pool of cards; multiplayer
League of Legends	Different combinations of heroes (and available skills) in fights; multiplayer
The Last of Us	Limited resources; AI-driven enemies; new environments
Mario Kart	Unique tracks; mystery power-ups; kart customisation
Overwatch	Unique maps; different team compositions; multiplayer
Rocket League	Semi-unpredictable ball physics; multiplayer
Tetris	Randomised tetrominoes of varying shape/ size

3.2.7.3 Champions

Simply put: your Spark should be capable of creating an experience where it is possible for players to achieve incredible feats others can aspire to. This is not just for the benefit of said player, but rather for those who are watching them.

In addition to creating a highly compelling sense of group identity, thanks to certain cells in the brain known as mirror neurons,[16] viewers can actually feel like they are playing a game they are watching. This can allow viewers to internalise their entertainment and experience the emotions they would feel were they doing it themselves.[17]

Those of you who have felt the thrill of a rollercoaster simply by standing next to one, watching and listening to others enjoy ('enjoy'...) their ride, will undoubtedly be capable of relating to this sensation – which is precisely why watching someone recreate the Taj Mahal in *Minecraft* or achieve a 15-strong killstreak in *Call of Duty* can be so compelling.

3.3 WORKSHOP TASK

3.3.1 Chapter Highlights

- It is important that you take the time to validate a Spark before diving straight into developing them further – be it on paper or through a prototype to ensure you are building on top of something solid.
- Validating concepts through prototyping can be an expensive exercise, particularly for more complex or nuanced concepts, whose effectiveness may require a larger slice of the experience to be developed before they can be accurately evaluated.
- The Lightning Rod offers a series of questions to ask of your Spark before writing up a full pitch for it: questions (a.k.a. *rungs*) that I believe numerous existing CVCs answer positively to which I myself have used to great effect when writing video game pitches.

  - Rung #1: Does Your High-level Concept Meet Your Design Restrictions?

    - While the high-level concept phase of a Spark's creation can be a lot of fun, the strength of any Spark is ultimately the sum of its parts, which includes the design restrictions this process began with. Check in with your core experience to make sure it meets them – especially Key Restrictions 1 and 2.

- Rung #2: Does It Do Anything First Or Best?

  - Ask yourself if your Spark's high-level concept could offer an entirely unique experience – *Minecraft* being a good example – or deliver upon an existing core experience better tailored for the audience it inherently attracts.

- Rung #3: Does It Offer Room For Player Improvement?

  - The more time a player can sink into the video game created from your Spark in a bid to further master its mechanics and witness the results of that mastery firsthand – the better! Collection and task completion are all very well and good, of course, but the process of learning how to play – and play better – is vital for any CVC because, if I've learned anything after close to a decade of designing video games, it's that above feeling powerful or free, players like to feel smart.

- Rung #4: Does The Puzzle Match The Player?

  - Every video game is essentially a puzzle for someone else to figure out – albeit (at times) rather complex or even subtle puzzles! Consider whether the style of puzzle your Spark would offer will be capable of attracting and being solved by its intended audience.

- Rung #5: Does It Exhibit Conduciveness?

  - Conducive design is the process of looking for natural evolutions in a video game's design decisions – which (if maintained) leads to a state of Harmony. Some Sparks will be inherently more conducive design-friendly than others.

- Rung #6: Does It Prioritise Gameplay?

  - While there are exceptions to the rule, the majority of CVCs (be it *Minecraft* or *Counter-Strike*) tend to focus on great gameplay over everything else – games that are primarily played for learning their mechanics rather than spoon-fed narrative rewards. Unless you are confident that your storytelling skills are red hot – ask yourself if your Spark primarily focuses on the former.

- Rung #7: Does It Recreate The Colosseum Effect?

  - Considering the majority of today's CVCs (and indeed older CVCs when people used to huddle around a single arcade machine) are just as compelling to watch as they are to play, try to determine to what extent the video game your Spark would produce would offer suspense, variety and champions to emerge.

3.3.2 Reader Assignment

1. Send your Spark down the Lightning Rod to see how many rungs it passes through successfully – and be honest with yourself about how well it passes through them!

   a. If your Spark answers positively to the majority of the rungs, then by my reckoning, you may have a CVC on your hands – proceed to Chapter 4.

   b. If your Spark does not answer positively to the majority of the rungs – you have three choices:

      i. Option 1: Give yourself a well-earned pat on the back for all your hard work so far and ask yourself why your Spark wasn't able to make it all the way down the Lightning Rod – is there anything about it that you can change for a better result? Be it your design restrictions, the high-level concept, or both.

      ii. Option 2: Start again from the beginning of Chapter 2. While you will very likely grow attached to your high-level concepts and Sparks, the whole point of this process is that (beyond being relatively cheap) it is intended to provide you with a strong and reliable foundation that offers a higher chance of CVC creation. Assuming you are willing to trust this process and believe in the value it has offered my own pitches to-date, don't be afraid to start from scratch – I promise you that the Spark you're holding on to is far from your best work.

      iii. Option 3: Ignore what may be red flags and push forward regardless. Whether it's because you don't fully trust the vision-crafting process, or because you firmly believe in your Spark, continuing on to Chapter 4 for advice on how to articulate and flesh it out further prior to beginning development is an entirely valid choice. Trust your gut!

NOTES

1. www.polygon.com/features/2014/1/20/5227582/the-rise-of-the-jump
2. www.arcade-museum.com/game_detail.php?game_id=9787
3. https://ultimateclassicrock.com/donkey-kong-1981-game/
4. https://refreshingwednesday.com/2019/07/08/mastery-requires-boredom/
5. www.pocketgamer.com/candy-crush-saga/how-many-levels-are-there/
6. https://talent.gamehouse.com/inspiration/psychology-cognitive-flow
7. www.psychologytoday.com/us/blog/freedom-learn/201803/sense-and-nonsense-about-video-game-addiction
8. https://youtu.be/yuOObGjCA7Q
9. https://youtu.be/yuOObGjCA7Q
10. www.youtube.com/watch?v=aEYBGL6L234
11. www.giantbomb.com/headshot/3015-85/
12. www.metacritic.com/game/switch/celeste
13. https://kenzie.snhu.edu/blog/what-is-rubber-duck-debugging/
14. www.forbes.com/sites/mattgardner1/2023/02/09/here-are-the-ten-most-popular-games-for-streamers-in-2022/
15. www.bps.org.uk/psychologist/allure-mysteries
16. www.psychreg.org/psychology-watching-sports-what-fans-get-watching-football/
17. www.mic.com/articles/104224/science-reveals-why-we-re-obsessed-with-watching-sports

Chapter 4

Articulation

4.1 CHAPTER INTRODUCTION

Before we get started on the beginning of the end, if you're still here by this point, I would like to pause for just a moment and sincerely thank you for your time and interest – not to mention picking up this book in the first place! I sincerely hope you have garnered at least a couple of useful insights and practices along the way that have helped you understand the importance of video game pitch design and how to tackle them with both confidence and competence. But we're not quite done yet . . .

As is my general experience with titles for anything, be it a video game pitch or otherwise, the title of this book evolved over time. What I really should have called it is something along the lines of *How to Sculpt a Video Game*, but I agree with friends and colleagues who were less enamoured with this idea that it might have been somewhat confusing, regardless of my already liberal use of metaphors and similes throughout this book. . . . That being said, as undeniably pretentious titles go, it would have been fairly indicative of how I personally see video game pitching: a process that involves gradually whittling a corporeal block of nothingness into a recognizable shape that achieves greater detail over time – as opposed to simply catching something fully formed out of thin air and bottling it up. The trouble is that, being entirely invisible to all others but the sculptor, it means that one of the biggest challenges is not only producing a well-defined sculpture but also successfully communicating what it looks like to everyone else – 'successful' in this context being defined by how accurately its image is relayed. An act which, as we'll touch on, can prove to be extremely helpful as part of the sculpting process in-and-of itself. For some, depending on their skill set, this invisible entity can be drawn into life,

DOI: 10.1201/9781003269632-4

whereas others can code it into existence – both a means of providing this otherwise invisible creation with a tangible form. But for those like me, we are entirely reliant on the power of clear and compelling words alone to capture and convey our conceptual creations and, just as there are best practices around the former two (i.e. knowledge and experience that can improve the outcome) there are surely best practices around the latter, which this chapter aims to cover.

This phase of the process is one that many seem to find the most challenging – and with good reason. It is my experience that clearly communicating an idea to others can prove to be considerably more difficult than conceptualising the idea in the first place, which is entirely understandable, considering the many intimidating questions it can present:

- 'How much detail is too much detail?'
- 'What exactly should I say – and in what order?'
- 'How should it be visually presented?'

But all these questions pale in comparison to the most important question you may have when it comes to writing out your pitch: why bother? For some of you, particularly solo developers with the skills to create working prototypes and less of a need to share your vision via documentation, this phase of the process may appear to be somewhat less important now that you have a Spark you are feeling happy and confident with. That being said, the significance of strong written communication skills for any designer (especially those working in the industry) aside, there are several key reasons as to why the articulation of a pitch can be vitally important – regardless of your circumstances.

The first of these is concept development. Throughout my career, I have worked on countless pitches, features and systems and can say with complete certainty that they have all shared the same requirement: the need for thinking things through. What may seem like the perfect idea or solution at first glance can be far less effective or simple as it initially appears – however excited it might make you. Don't get me wrong: feeling genuinely excited over an idea is a rare, wonderful thing and a potential indicator that you're headed in the right direction. After all, if you're not having fun creating something, how could it possibly receive the love and care required to make it truly special for someone else to experience? But this excitement can often result in making a similar mistake to one outlined by Netflix founder Marc Randolph when it comes to hiring:

> Hiring too fast is like skipping steps in a recipe – it might seem efficient at first, but the end result can be disastrous.
>
> – Marc Randolph[1]

Do not mistake that feeling of excitement for confirmation that your design is without issue, or even solves the problems you are attempting to answer and risk making the mistake of 'skipping steps', however efficient it may seem – measure twice; cut once.

What makes a pitch's importance especially significant is that, in being the foundation, the harder and more costly it can become to change over time. For instance, if one were to begin developing a video game based on a pitch that utilised a third-person camera, this fundamental aspect of said pitch would incur numerous design and technical decisions that would be rendered completely obsolete were this aspect to be changed – requiring entirely new solutions to replace them. Solutions whose cost and complications could potentially even end a project.

I have often found that writing out design documentation – be it a proposal, spec or pitch – is the best way of identifying potential pitfalls or considerations you hadn't previously identified and is guaranteed to result in a stronger video game. As Kidlin's Law puts it:

> If you can write a problem down clearly, then it is already half solved.
>
> – Kidlin[2]

The second reason to write out your pitch, regardless of circumstance, is concept definition. Thinking an idea through is one thing – but explaining it is quite another! You could have the best video game pitch in the world, but (assuming you aren't able to create it entirely on your own) if you are unable to explain it in a clear and compelling way to others, it can be rendered somewhat powerless. The importance of how something is conveyed is by no means limited to the written word: a study by the UCLA showed that, when presenting, the non-verbal component of said presentation accounted for 93% of audience impact compared to the 7% created by the content itself.[3] Think of a video game pitch as an opportunity to perfectly capture an immutable version of your vision through carefully chosen words that accurately represents your concept – which is especially important when a single ill-placed word of any description can make all the difference between boredom and buy-in. As the renowned author of timeless classics *The Adventures of Tom Sawyer* (1876) and *Adventures of Huckleberry Finn* (1884) once put it:

> The difference between the almost right word and the right word is really a large matter – it's the difference between the lightning bug and the lightning.
>
> – Mark Twain[4]

The third and final reason is concept distribution. The true power of any idea, be it for a video game or otherwise, often lies in its capacity to spread. While it may be true that there is typically no better source of truth than "straight from the horse's mouth", being able to give someone an asset capable of clearly communicating your vision in its entirety (rather than just a tiny and far from representative part of it) which can in turn be passed on to others may provide your pitch with a greater chance of taking flight through its ability to be shared.

Now that we have covered the why, let's focus on the what – or more specifically what's important when it comes to writing a video game pitch document.

When it comes to writing any kind of design documentation, be it a video game pitch or feature specification, there are *Four Horsemen of the A-doc-alypse* (sorry – I genuinely couldn't help myself) that represent your greatest challenges to overcome:

1. Assumption: When the content leads to incorrect assumptions
2. Boredom: When the content causes loss of interest
3. Confusion: When the content causes uncertainty
4. Doubt: When the content fails to inspire confidence

This chapter is therefore dedicated to providing you with advice that I myself have learned throughout my career on how best to go about developing and expressing your pitch on paper, ranging from document structure and formatting to key sections and pro tips, all of which should help you keep said horsemen at bay. There are countless forms of pitch document out there across the video game industry – all of which will have their benefits and drawbacks. As I have mentioned before, what I am about to outline is quite simply what I have personally experienced success with when it comes to video game pitching, which I very much hope will be the case for you too!

It took me a while to figure out how best to approach this particular part of the process in a way that didn't involve me basically writing a second book, as well as offer insights that could be applied to pitch document creation in general, regardless of the format you choose. To that end, we'll be discussing how to tackle the very first page of a pitch document, before covering several topics that relate to everything else that comes afterwards.

4.2 THE FIRST PAGE

In an age of fifteen-second video clips and 280-character tweets where attention spans can be short-lived and every second is more valuable than ever before, as you might expect, the first page of a pitch document can simultaneously be the most challenging and important page to get right.

I have often found that new pitchers make a strong attempt to cram as much text as possible into their first page, which I can certainly understand the rationale for, considering it is the first thing their reader is going to see and the fear they may not read any further than that! But as we will be covering very shortly, when it comes to your first page, less is absolutely more.

It is also worth mentioning that you may end up writing the final version of your first page last – after you have written up the rest of your pitch document. This is because, by the time you have finished writing the entire pitch document, you will probably have a much better understanding of the pitch and in turn find it far easier to summarise. You can't summarise a story effectively until you know the story in full.

Either way, let's take a look at a breakdown of what I typically include on page one of a pitch document (as illustrated in Figure 4.1), which I have repeatedly found strikes an effective balance between clarity, brevity and visual appeal. As you can see, page one consists of five key parts, four of which will be individually covered in the following sub-chapters – the Razor having been covered already in Chapter 2.

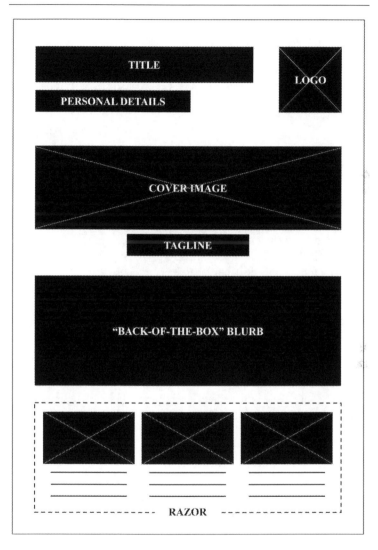

Figure 4.1 Page one – layout and key components.

4.2.1 Title

Odds are that the title of your pitch document will be one of the first things your reader sees, which basically means it is the most important aspect of your first page and sometimes the most challenging! As the founder of Lunarch Studios once put it:

> Naming *Prismata* was probably the hardest decision we ever had to make [throughout four years of development] . . . I imagine that it might feel similar to naming a first child, except there are lawyers involved.

> – Elyot Grant[5]

This is not to say that coming up with the perfect title is more important than a thoroughly thought-out and well-written pitch. A strong title can, however, most definitely help ensure your pitch creates a strong and memorable initial impression. Like any first impression, it can be entirely misplaced or inaccurate, but it is nevertheless still a first impression – which you won't get a second chance at!

While the title may (and most likely will) change between pitch and eventual product, this does not mean it is unimportant, namely because it offers you the opportunity to begin building a picture of your pitch in the mind's eye of your reader as quickly and clearly as possible.

When confronted with the challenge of creating a pitch title, there are several factors I typically bear in mind that we are just about to cover, but in my opinion the most important hallmark of a strong pitch title is quite simple: 'will it help the reader build a better picture of the experience I am trying to describe?' – particularly with regard to core gameplay, intended audience and overall tone. Is it about platforming or shooting? Is it for younger players or older players? Is it cute or mature?

With that in mind, the majority of video game titles (CVCs included) typically, but by no means always, relate to:

1. A key event that occurs in the video game – for example, *Journey*; *Mass Effect*; *Death's Door*
2. An important place in the video game – for example, *Halo*; *Silent Hill*; *Sea of Thieves*
3. The main character(s) of the video game – for example, *Shovel Knight*; *Mario*; *Max Payne*
4. The core gameplay of the video game – for example, *Minecraft*; *Grand Theft Auto*; *It Takes Two*

My advice would be to choose a title that favours function over fashion and focuses on options 3 and 4: a title that attempts to convey the gameplay of your pitch above all else. CVCs such as *Tomb Raider* or *Mario Kart* are great examples which instantly achieve this and immediately conjure a sense of what the experience will primarily revolve around – which is precisely what you should be aiming for. Portmanteaus (i.e. the fusion of multiple words to form a new word) such as *Minecraft* can also be effective!

This is not to say that titles like *The Last of Us* or *Mario* are not powerful titles in their own right – especially when coupled with their complementary box-art and impressive trailers! But it is important to acknowledge that these titles, while perhaps somewhat suggestive of the intended audience, would arguably struggle to create an immediate sense of their gameplay to anyone completely unfamiliar with them.

Furthermore, a strong title should seek to strike a balance between being memorable and unique, without instilling complex spelling or pronunciation that could make it difficult for a prospective reader to find again in their inbox or feel embarrassed to attempt saying out loud. To that end, homophonic titles – titles which utilise words that sound similar but have entirely different meanings and spellings – are also worth avoiding, be it 'affect' and 'effect' or 'forspoken' and 'forsaken'.

You may have also noticed that the majority of CVC titles are constructed from between two to four syllables, which Alen Brew of *Branding Business* calls *The Law of 3 Syllables*.

> There is an unwritten Law of Three Syllables that explains why New York (two syllables) gets its full name while Los Angeles (four syllables) is more popularly referred to as 'LA.' Likewise, Detroit is always Detroit, but Philadelphia is 'Philly.'
>
> – Alan Brew[6]

Naturally there are exceptions – as is the case with every rule – but whether it is because they are easier to remember or catchier to say, I would recommend aiming for between two to four syllables when it comes to your video game pitch's title.

4.2.2 Tagline

If your pitch document were a three-course meal, then taglines could essentially be considered as the amuse bouche: a small bite that leaves your reader wanting more and creates an instant expectation of what is to come.

Table 4.1 Tagline Examples

CVC (A–Z)	Tagline Example
Elden Ring	'Zelda: Breath of the Wild – for adults'
Fall Guys: Ultimate Knockout	'Takeshi's Castle – the game'[7]
Sonic Frontiers	'Open-world Sonic'

It is a singular, typically reference or verb driven, high-level sentence capable of instantly explaining the entire game, which I fully appreciate sounds like an impossible task at first glance, so let's take a quick look at some potential and completely hypothetical taglines for existing CVCs in Table 4.1.

In the case of *Fall Guys: Ultimate Knock-out*, '*Takeshi's Castle* – the game' (assuming the reader is familiar with the reference) instantly offers a clear overall impression of the game's experience, rather than attempting to encapsulate every single detail of the video game's gameplay or story, which is very much the hallmark of a strong tagline – for example:

- Something silly
- Something obstacle-course based
- Something with lots of players
- Something with hilarious (and somewhat painful-looking) failures
- Something game-show themed

As you may have also noticed and as I briefly touched on beforehand, each of our examples intentionally uses references that a reader is likeliest to have a pre-existing understanding of, primarily because the effectiveness of any reference ultimately relies upon its familiarity. In other words: if you try explaining something to someone using a reference they are unfamiliar with, it won't help them understand what you are trying to say, however accurate your reference may be. To that end, if you happen to know of a reference that perfectly reflects the experience your video game pitch intends to capitalise on but is relatively niche or unknown, I would highly advise looking for an alternate reference – especially if you intend to share your pitch with others.

The examples provided also primarily revolve around the core activity of their experience and attempt to succinctly communicate what the player will do in the video game – rather than what will happen to them! Don't get me wrong: narrative can certainly contextualise and rationalise mechanics to create a potentially stronger pitch/video game! *Portal 2* is still one of my all-time favourite practical examples of this: leaning into the sci-fi nature of its signature mechanic to imbue it with believability and meaning – a prime example of conducive design. Even *Mario's* fantastical and (between sentient mushrooms and princess-stealing dinosaurs) borderline nonsensical premise serves its gameplay requirements perfectly, allowing for all manner of creative platforming challenges that require little contextualisation, thanks to them existing in a beautifully bizarre gameworld. However, when it comes to a tagline, never forget that one of the most important differences (if not the most important of all) between video games and other forms of media entertainment is that video games offer consumers autonomy: the power to do something, decide when they want to do it and having an emotional reaction to that command. They are an active form of engagement rather than a passive one, such as a book or a movie, the enjoyment of which ultimately boils down to making a button fun to press and in turn making decisions that are of interest to the types of people the video game is designed for.[8] In short: I urge you to keep your tagline focused on capturing the overall gameplay experience of your pitch rather than trying to summarise any form of story that might be accompanying it – however proud or excited you are about said story.

To illustrate this point with an example, let's say you were pitching the very first *Mario* game and offered the following tagline: 'Rescue a princess from a dinosaur as a plumber'. While this is a (somewhat) technically accurate description of the game's premise, it doesn't really tell us anything about the gameplay and is potentially even misleading if one were to assume it does! Based on this tagline alone, I am fairly confident that someone completely unfamiliar with your pitch would be unable to visualise the experience we know *Mario* to be, nor accurately comprehend what they would be capable of doing in the game . . .

To offer an example of what I would consider to be a weak tagline with this in mind:

> *NEON WHITE* is a lightning fast first-person action game about exterminating demons in Heaven.
>
> *– Annapurna*[9]

This particular quote was taken from a tweet, the purpose of which was likely to market Angel Matrix's truly fantastic *Neon White*, which I own a copy of myself and would highly recommend! Nevertheless, it is a great example of how I often see taglines written by new pitchers, in the sense that (while again being technically accurate) it is nigh-impossible to visualise the actual – and very compelling – gameplay something like *Neon White* offers.

4.2.3 Cover Image

As the old saying goes 'a picture says a thousand words', so I always like to include a cover image as part of my pitch documents, being the highly visual creatures we are!

I appreciate that not everyone (myself included) is an artist, knows an artist they can reach out to for support or has the resources required to hire one. Nevertheless, I strongly suggest that you find a way of including a high-quality cover image in your pitch document, given that just one piece of key art (i.e. artwork that essentially creates a fake screenshot of your video game) can offer both you and others an imme-diate and very literal picture of whatever experience your pitch intends to offer – not to mention a little production value. Consider it a small investment for what will more than likely prove to be an incredibly valuable aid.

That aside, you may be wondering what your pitch document's cover image should focus on, be it gameplay, the main character, an in-game location or something else entirely. Based on my own pitches, particularly the ones that have seen greater success and uptake, I would argue that an effective cover image typically incorporates four corner-stones (see Figure 4.2) which draw inspiration from the best example of cover images available: video game box covers!

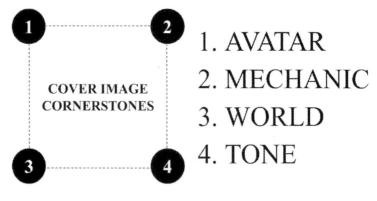

Figure 4.2 Cover image cornerstones.

Considering the fact that almost all video games allow players to step into the shoes of a fictional character, who also almost always just so happens to be the most important individual in its fictional universe, it is unsurprising that video game boxes have included this cornerstone of cover images for decades. Ensure that your cover image allows would-be readers, yourself included, to clearly understand the type of role they would assume in your pitch's experience and how that role would make them feel. Most importantly, be it a dinky race car or burly armour-clad marine, try to consider what manner of avatar would appeal to your given target audience. Design for what your players will like – rather than for what you want them to like.

Even when a video game doesn't feature a central fantasy – a role for the player to assume in your gameworld – they always feature something the player can do, bringing us to the next cornerstone of pitch document cover images, which is 'mechanic'. Whether it is including a firearm, sword, pick-axe, portal gun in the avatar's hand or showing tetrominoes slotting into place, your cover image must – without fail – indicate the primary mechanic of your pitch in order to indicate not just what role the player will assume but, most importantly, what they will be capable of doing in your video game.

It is also important to convey where your pitch will transport players to: is it a happy world or a sad one? Is it a fantastical world – or one rooted in reality? A safe space – or one fraught with peril? This particular cornerstone can be highly effective at allowing viewers to quickly surmise the general premise of a new video game, as well as indicate 'tone' which is largely communicated by visual style and colour schemes to provide an immediate sense of who your pitch is intended for. Try comparing the box-art of Nintendo's *Kirby and the Forgotten Land* with something like Naughty Dog's *The Last of Us* – both of which are highly effective at communicating the tones and subsequent intended audiences of the experiences on offer.

4.2.4 Back-of-the-Box Blurb

Last but not least we have what I like to call the 'back-of-the-box blurb'.

As any of you who play video games will probably know, whenever you pick up a video game box and turn it over, or enter its listing on an online store, you are typically offered a relatively concise description of the game. This is essentially what the first page of your pitch document needs to contain – and nail.

The idea here is to simultaneously offer your reader just enough information to clearly explain the high-level experience of your pitch while making them want to know more. Easy, right? Having written dozens of these blurbs throughout my career across various studios and pitches, I have personally experienced the best results (in terms of pitch document uptake and follow-through) by separating it into two parts, both of which serve different purposes.

4.2.4.1 Part 1

This initial part of the back-of-the-box blurb is typically a single sentence that focuses on highlighting:

- Genre
- Intended target audience
- Tone

You may have noticed that the aforementioned list doesn't mention gameplay, but don't worry, that's what Part 2 is for!

In order to provide a clearer sense of how Part 1 might look in practice, here are some hypothetical examples (see Table 4.2) of how I myself would write it for several very different CVCs, so as to illustrate the similarities in approach regardless of the distinct experience they offer for very different intended target audiences:

Table 4.2 Back-of-the-Box-Blurb Examples (Part 1)

Elden Ring	*Elden Ring* is a single-player, hack'n'slash, open-world RPG adventure intended for a mature audience that will transport them to a dark and epic fantasy experience.
Overwatch	*Overwatch* is a vibrant team-based competitive first-person shooter, featuring role-driven gameplay that offers players personality-packed sci-fi heroes to master as part of a bright and highly stylised universe intended to achieve broad appeal.
Super Mario Odyssey	*Super Mario Odyssey* is a family-friendly, single-player, 3rd-person platformer designed for a broad audience, boasting a traditionally upbeat "*Mario* soul" and optional objectives, allowing younger audiences to progress while providing more mature audiences with opportunities for greater mastery.

4.2.4.2 Part 2

The second part of our back-of-the-box blurb is a carefully constructed paragraph, separate from Part 1, that focuses exclusively on gameplay – specifically the aspects of your pitch's gameplay that make it either unique or interesting.

This is your opportunity to communicate the best bits of your pitch's gameplay, so don't hold back, or worry about keeping your best ideas for last. Focus on trying to make it as clear as possible why this particular pitch would be fun for the intended audience to play – but don't worry about trying to tell them every single detail you can either. Be strict with yourself and remember that this text still has to fit on our first page, so be economical with your words and feel free to crop the size of your cover image if desperately needed. All we are trying to do at this point is grab the reader's attention and get them invested in our pitch. If we are able to grab them by the first page, odds are, they will read enough of the pitch to eventually learn about all the other 'best bits' you have planned!

Once again, practical and hypothetical examples have been provided in Table 4.3 using the same CVCs as before, but this time for Part 2 of our back-of-the-box blurb.

Table 4.3 Back-of-the-Box-Blurb Examples (Part 2)

Elden Ring	Wield all manner of hard-earned and powerful weapons or spells at your disposal to vanquish any who stand in your way, allowing you to create and evolve unique combat styles that suit your playstyle while exploring a vast, calamity-stricken open world where every second is another temptation to stray from the beaten path. A world filled with enormous and unique locations, obscured hidden areas to scour through, environmental storytelling and a wide variety of foes ranging from tiny to towering in a bid to become the Elden Lord.
	Prepare to die.

(Continued)

Table 4.3 (Continued)

Overwatch	Become one of several highly distinct heroes boasting unique firearms and cooldown-based abilities to experience the thrill of being part of a synergised team that must combine their skills and work together in order to secure victory. An experience that is organically and subtly enforced through distinct team roles (DPS; Tank; Support) suited for different types of player and objective-focused matches to provide lighting rods for team collaboration. Welcome to *Overwatch*.
Super Mario Odyssey	Wielding *Cappy* – a new companion that allows *Mario* to *possess* enemies and utilise their unique abilities to solve puzzles or traverse the environment in new ways – players will embark on a joyous journey across several vibrant and colourful mini open-worlds, from bustling cities to tropical beaches, each packed with secret areas, distinct platforming challenges and hidden collectibles. Let's a'go!

4.3 BEYOND PAGE 1

The aim of a pitch document, beyond page one, is essentially to expand upon the exciting aspects of your pitch that you will have undoubtedly mentioned in your back-of-the-box blurb (see Figure 4.3).

This is precisely why I advised not worrying too much about trying to explain everything as quickly as possible in your first page and is a

> *Super Mario Odyssey* is a family-friendly, single-player, 3rd-person platformer designed for a broad audience, boasting a traditionally upbeat "*Mario* soul" and **optional objectives**, allowing younger audiences to progress while providing more mature audiences with **opportunities for greater mastery**.
>
> Wielding **'Cappy'- a new companion that allows *Mario* to "possess" enemies and utilise their unique abilities to solve puzzles or traverse the environment in new ways**, players will embark on a joyous journey across **several vibrant and colourful mini open-worlds**, from bustling cities to tropical beaches, each packed with secret areas, **distinct platforming challenges** and **hidden collectibles**.

Figure 4.3 Back-of-the-box blurb: key call-outs.

common lesson of writing design documentation: you needn't explain a term or concept immediately – just so long as you explain it somewhere eventually!

Regardless of whatever type of video game you are pitching, there are three facets of a pitch document that will always be important to consider:

1. Structure: the sections included in your pitch document and their ordering
2. Formatting: the visual layout of your pitch document's presentation
3. Writing style: the way in which your pitch document's content is communicated

Let's take a look at each of these facets in greater detail.

4.3.1 Structure

The importance of structure in a pitch document could best be likened to the room layout of a building's floor plan. To aid me in this metaphorical comparison I have put my unquestionably questionable artistic talents to use again with the diagram in Figure 4.4.

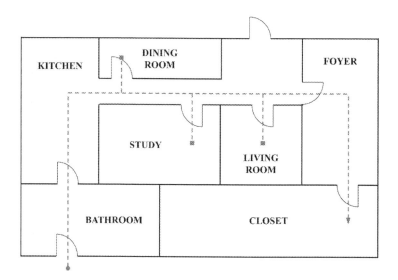

Figure 4.4 The importance of structure.

I would like to think we can all agree that this structure is – for want of a much fancier word befitting of someone entrusted with writing a book – bad. While I admittedly know next to nothing about architecture, I think it would be safe to say that most guests would be either confused or unhappy with this structure for several reasons, such as:

- The bathroom being the first room they would be in upon entering the building . . .
- The kitchen sharing a door with the bathroom – which doesn't seem very sanitary . . .
- The foyer (out of seven possible rooms) being the sixth room they would reach . . .
- The closet being the largest room in the house and likely not the best use of the space available considering its utility in comparison to other rooms

Think of these imaginary rooms as the sections and subsections of your pitch document – and the entire document itself as an open floor. The order in which you present information, as well as the amount of space you dedicate to differing types of information, can seriously help or hinder when it comes to navigating and understanding a pitch – as well as its overall impact. As highlighted by Nancy Duarte in her exceptional 2010 TED Talk *The Secret Structure of Great Talks*, the power and significance of structure can even be seen throughout numerous notable speeches, from those of Steve Jobs to Martin Luther King – further highlighting the substantial importance of structure.[10]

The 'rooms' I myself typically include in my own pitch documents – as well as how many A4 pages I dedicate to each of them – includes:

A. Key USPs (0.5 pages)
B. Look and Feel (0.25 pages)
C. Game Loops (1 page)
D. Who/What, Where and Why (1–2 pages per topic)
E. Magic Moments (0.5 pages)
F. Lifetime Roadmap (0.5 pages)

While it has been my experience that these page-counts have often struck the sweet spot between creating intrigue, offering clarity and maintaining brevity, I should probably emphasise that the quicker you can communicate your pitch in an engaging way without sacrificing said clarity, the better! It is also worth noting that, just because I myself have typically found success in using the aforementioned structure (which I offer in the hope that it helps you too) it does not mean that this is the only way to structure your pitch document. Writing a pitch is ultimately a process that involves understanding the design challenge that needs to be solved, establishing a solution for said challenge and communicating that solution in the most effective and user-friendly way. That said, I have certainly found the given structure to be fairly effective, regardless of the design challenge at hand.

Furthermore, should you choose to follow the structure provided, this also does not mean that you must write them out chronologically. Instead, I would highly recommend that you jump straight into the sections of your pitch that excite you most and are clearest in your head, if only to maintain momentum.

With these points in mind – let's touch on each of the aforementioned sections!

4.3.1.1 USPs

For anyone unfamiliar with this term, 'USP' is an acronym that stands for 'Unique Selling Point': three to four aspects of your design, described at a high level, that you believe only your video game can offer, would resonate or be of interest to your intended target audience and prove most important to its overall success.

USPs can include anything about a video game's design, be it related to mechanics, visuals, the relationships it aims to create between players and everything in-between, but in my experience USPs should ideally attempt to communicate how a design will deliver on the experience promised despite a player's best efforts to ruin their own fun because:

> Given the opportunity, players will optimise the fun out of a game. . . . One of the responsibilities of designers is to protect them [players] from themselves.
>
> – Soren Johnson/Sid Meier[11]

To elaborate on the latter: if a player discovers that rolling around is a faster means of in-game movement than running, odds are they'll resort to rolling everywhere, even if it goes against the fantasy they are meant to be fulfilling in your video game. One of my all-time favourite examples of highly considerate design-thinking in this regard comes from Rocksteady's *Batman: Arkham Asylum*, wherein the player's default movement of Batman is walking – not running. This may seem like an inconsequential decision, but make no mistake that this would have undoubtedly been an intentional one by Rocksteady, utilising a subtle and effective means of delivering on its core experience of being *The Batman* – someone you probably don't envision sprinting all over the place rather than predatorily walking with control and poise.

Just in case this example causes any confusion: don't mistake "player won't run by default" as a USP! While it may be the result or even part of an encompassing USP – for example, *Be The Batman* – it would in-and-of itself be far too low-level a detail for something as significant as a dedicated USP.

In order to provide practical examples that also illustrate just how distinct USPs can (and should) be, here are two sets of hypothetical USPs for two very different first-person shooter CVCs, which will quickly demonstrate how different their USPs could be despite belonging to the same genre (see Tables 4.4 to 4.5):

Table 4.4 USP Example: DOOM (2016)

USP Title	USP Body
The Joy Of (Constant) Movement	*DOOM (2016)* will feature fast-paced and fluid movement that makes players feel as quick and deadly as the Doom Marine himself – as well as constant reasons to keep moving in varied ways! Players will (literally) barely have time to blink as they blaze across battlefields running, jumping and weaving between dangers and obstacles alike.
Rock/Paper/ Shotgun	While all weapons in *DOOM (2016)* will feel powerful and deadly – all befitting of The Slayer – each firearm will offer unique and easy-to-identify pros and cons regarding enemy strengths and weaknesses, providing players with a sense of smartness and satisfaction when considering how best to solve combat challenges on-the-fly!
Push-forward Combat	Through the omission of go-to genre staples such as reloading, regenerating health and enemies who always give chase, players will be invited to embrace the brutal power of The Slayer: encouraging them to engage with enemies head-on to out-manoeuvre and out-gun them rather than cower behind terrain.

Table 4.5 USP Example: Overwatch

USP Title	USP Body
A Champion For Everyone	*Overwatch* will offer a wide variety of characters to play as across three distinct roles, providing different play-styles for different player-types as well as a broad range of inclusive representation. Champion diversity will also aid match variance – better ensuring no two matches are ever the same.
Clear Roles For Clear Goals	Champions in *Overwatch* will feature clear silhouettes, set weaponry and specific abilities, not only offering players new avenues of mastery with every character that allows them to better anticipate specific threats in the heat of battle and make more informed choices about them, but also ensuring no single player can *do everything* – further encouraging team-play in the pursuit of victory.
A Shooter For Anyone	Between the omission of *aiming-down-sights*, action-stopping ammo supply gathering and any form of gore, *Overwatch* will offer a highly approachable first-person shooter further bolstered by a bright and vibrant gameworld. Just because you don't have the best aim doesn't mean you shouldn't get to play a great first-person shooter!

4.3.1.2 Look and Feel

A quick comparison with an existing game's art-style, alongside a reference image or two, can do wonders for helping your reader further build a picture of your pitch in their head, whether it's cartoonish (e.g. *Super Mario Odyssey*), stylised (e.g. *Overwatch*), realistic (e.g. *The Last of Us*), somewhere in-between or something else entirely.

Communicating the intended and ideal aesthetic of your pitch can also help showcase your pitch's suitability for the target audience you have in mind – potentially creating a greater sense of confidence in your concept's prospective effectiveness as a product. For example, were someone attempting to pitch a shooter-style video game for young children with a highly realistic aesthetic, this particular combination could quite understandably raise some doubts, hence something like *Splatoon 3's* cartoonish and inviting presentation!

Never forget to consider the fact that you are attempting to pitch something for a specific intended target audience. Cooking a recipe for pasta-lovers that won't look anything like pasta is of course your call – but it's a risk to be taking nevertheless. Try to avoid simply choosing an aesthetic you like and instead consider what would stand the best chance of attracting the right types of player to your video game – the ones best suited for the type of experience it would offer.

As part of this section, it can also help to understand and verbalise how the resulting video game of your pitch would potentially 'feel' to play. There are two potential definitions of the word *feel* when it comes to video games – or indeed games in general:

1. How the game (not 'gameplay') will make you feel, and
2. How the gameplay (not 'game') will feel to play – and contribute towards the previous definition

To quickly underline the difference between these two definitions: between its narrative, soundtrack and mechanics, a video game could make the player feel like a powerful hero, whereas its actual game-feel could be heavy and floaty – as opposed to snappy and light.

When it comes to this particular section of your pitch I tend to focus on the second definition which, in tandem with your cover image, will only further solidify the mental picture being conjured in the mind's eye of your reader and should once again be tailored to the intended target audience of your pitch. It goes without saying that the final game-feel (and indeed aesthetic) of your video game may very well differ from the approaches you outline in your pitch, but just because you may go off-route during a journey doesn't mean that you shouldn't bother planning an initial route before setting off, which is a sure-fire way to quickly becoming lost. Not to mention the fact that anyone travelling with you will probably feel a lot more confident and excited about you knowing where you want to go – and how you intend to get there.

As several great books, *Game Feel* by Steve Swink (2008, Routledge)[12] being a particularly superb example and countless internet articles/videos will attest to, the matter of defining and understanding how game-feel is achieved on a deeper level is a subject entirely unto itself, which this book won't be attempting to cover in extensive detail for that very reason. That being said, here is a succinct and extremely high-level crash course in what I would argue typically comprises game-feel in video games, listed from A to Z:

- Audio: any/all auditory stimulus (e.g. SFX, music)
- Friction: any/all forces applied to the player or other in-game entities (e.g. gravity, acceleration)

- Timing: the duration of in-game actions and any abilities to affect said durations (e.g. animation cooldowns, hit-pause)
- Visuals: any/all on-screen elements (e.g. animations, VFX, feedback UI, camera shake)

While this list is by no means definitive considering how diverse game-feel's requirements can be across various genres, in my experience as a lifelong gamer and decade-long video game designer, it is these elements that typically play a major role in determining game-feel and the kind of topics to consider when thinking about 'feel' for your pitch. It may be difficult to determine precisely what your video game would actually feel like to play at this point, especially without anything tangible to test it out, but considering the sheer volume of reference material out there (i.e. existing video games), it should still be possible to offer a general sense of your pitch's eventual game-feel by comparing your pitch against said references and describing that feel on paper. You may be tempted to simply compare your video game's game-feel with a pre-existing reference and, if you're writing a pitch document for the benefit of you alone, this is a perfectly valid approach. However, if you happen to be writing it for a third party, bear in mind that your readers may not have played it – rendering that information useless.

Do a bit of research and pick up a video game or two that you think best matches your video game's future game-feel (all the while remembering who your intended target audience is and what you believe their needs to be) and consciously identify:

1. How it achieves the game-feel it does (bearing the crash-course above in mind)
2. How accurate/suitable a reference it is for your intended audience, what you would change and why

4.3.1.3 Game Loops

The term 'game feel', in the context of video game design, typically refers to the visual representation of how a video game will create a positive reinforcement system, providing the player with reward-incentivised challenges that simultaneously create and satiate anticipation – in the sense that the player receives the reward they were chasing while another presents itself (see Figures 4.5 to 4.6 of Table 4.6). This anticipation is typically what triggers dopamine in the brain[13]: the feel-good hormone responsible for creating a sense of pleasure that is part of our internal reward system.[14]

Table 4.6 Anticipation in Game Loops

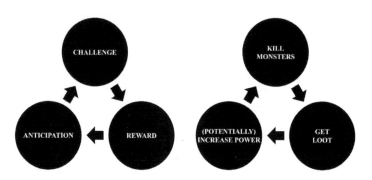

Figure 4.5 Game loop (high-level). *Figure 4.6* Game loop (in-game example).

Despite their apparent simplicity, getting a game loop down on paper can oftentimes be much easier said than done! Nevertheless, they can offer both you and readers immensely helpful summaries of your pitch, given that they succinctly communicate what I would argue is the shared DNA of general play:

- *D*ecisions to make
- *N*ew things to earn
- *A*ctions to master

They can also offer a clearer understanding of both the appeal and volume of a video game's medium- or long-term goals – which are often a big part of what influences players coming back!

Odds are that your video game will feature numerous decision points, rewards to earn and actions the player can master, so when it comes to including a game loop in your pitch document, I would recommend focusing solely on both the 'core' and 'meta loops' of your pitch – providing a loop for each one. To better explain what I mean by these terms, video games often consist of three distinct game loops (as illustrated in Figure 4.7), each of which could be defined by the frequency of their completion:

1. The Second-to-Second loop (completed the most frequently)
2. The Core loop
3. The Meta loop (completed the least frequently)

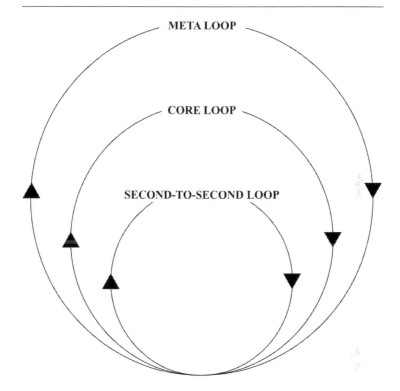

Figure 4.7 Game loops.

With these various types of game loop in mind, let's use *Super Mario 64* as an example of each of them in practice, mainly because (in terms of loops) it's relatively easy to break down and illustrate what each of them focuses on (see Table 4.7).

Table 4.7 Super Mario 64 Game Loops (Second-to-Second; Core; Meta)

Second-To-Second	Core	Meta
Challenge:	**Challenge:**	**Challenge:**
Jump correctly	Reach end of level	Unlock new levels
. . . In order to . . .	. . . In order to . . .	. . . In order to . . .
Reward:	**Reward:**	**Reward:**
Avoid dangers	Earn Stars	Have more Stars to earn
. . . In order to . . .	. . . In order to . . .	. . . In order to . . .
Anticipation:	**Anticipation:**	**Anticipation:**
Reach end of level	Unlock new levels	Collect all the Stars

As with many practices in the video games industry, people approach game loops in a variety of different ways, in terms of both the steps involved and their visual representation, which can make understanding what they should include even more confusing! Thankfully, after several instances of trying to explain game loops to others during pitch mentorship or junior designer support, I landed on a particular structure that has often helped with this learning curve (see Figure 4.8):

For whatever reason, I have often found that this waterfall-style game loop (named after the fact it travels vertically instead of circularly) is a little easier to get to grips with and in getting a game loop down on paper – the fact they fit much better on an A4 page is just an added bonus! Figure 4.9 offers a quick example of how something like *Super Mario Odyssey* might look, as a game loop, using this format to quickly communicate the decisions, goals and outcomes a player is typically offered from a second-to-second to meta level:

If you take anything away from this section (other than my recommendation to capture a game loop or two in your pitch of course) when it comes to understanding game loops and their importance – it would be this:

1. Use in-game rewards to teach the player how to play
2. Teach the player how to play in order to form new habits
3. Form new habits in order to engage and retain the player
4. Engage and retain the player to achieve cognitive flow[15]

Figure 4.8 Waterfall-style game loop – Example A.

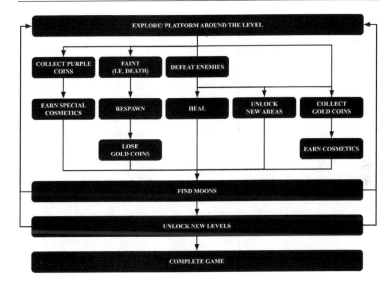

Figure 4.9 Waterfall-style game loop – Example B.

4.3.1.4 Who/What, Where & Why

Throughout the dozens of pitches I have written throughout my career, particularly the earlier . . . less informed . . . pitch documents, it occurred to me that readers almost always wanted answers to the same three questions:

1. 'Who will I be in the video game – and what can I (they) do?'
2. 'Where will I go in the video game – and how will that impact gameplay?'
3. 'Why will I keep playing the video game – and how will this improve my experience?'

As a result, I began structuring pitch documents beyond USPs, Look/ Feel and Game Loops using the latter three section headers, which I am pleased to say led to some of the strongest pitches I have written – in terms of uptake and how far they progressed.

Think back to when you were a small child. Odds are you played similar make-believe games just like everyone else! Games wherein you assumed a role other than your own – be it a policeman or a super-hero or (at the risk of figuratively repeating myself) a parent. These imagination-driven games also probably took place somewhere and like a tumbling snowball gathered new rules along the way as the game developed and evolved until, eventually, it reached its conclusion – or another game was conceived! The game itself may have involved you at the behest of someone else, or have been devised by you specifically, be it a solo or group affair – not to mention cooperative or competitive. I have long believed that this dynamic is essentially what video games tap into, the key difference being you are always stepping into some-one else's make-believe reality that doesn't and cannot benefit from the flexibility or on-the-fly development of childhood play, but the same things still matter to those involved regardless. Participants still need to enjoy the core fantasy they are being assigned; they still need to reso-nate with the type of world they are being transported to; and they need a reason to keep playing – typically because they are good (and being told they are good) at the game! Try to bear this in mind when writing out answers to each of the aforementioned key questions.

When writing out each section, start off with what is essentially a summarised answer, emboldening any key terms that come up along the way. Each of these bold key terms should receive their own sub-sections below the summary, allowing the reader to not only better understand these terms, but more importantly avoid the reader from being bombarded with information overload.

It is also vitally important to note that, when writing out each of these sub-sections, always try to focus on how they will further facili-tate and support gameplay. Using *Mario* as an example, simply stating 'players will play as an Italian Plumber who can jump' – while techni-cally true – is far from helpful or even particularly reflective of just how nuanced and interesting Mario's abilities actually are. Such a sub-section would ideally take the time to instead explain the intricacies of how Mario's jump works, be it chain-jumps leading to higher peaks, or height being linked to button-press duration. Shallow descriptions of equally shallow gameplay will undoubtedly fail to excite or inspire!

4.3.1.5 Magic Moments

Simply put, magic moments are short paragraphs that describe memo-rable events the player would experience in the video game you are pitching, which can be a useful way of clearly communicating what makes your pitch unique, compelling and suitable for the intended tar-get audience.

The magic moments you write, as well as where this particular section is placed in the pitch document, revolve around what is referred to as the Peak-End Rule:

> [A] cognitive bias that impacts how people remember past events. Intense positive or negative moments (the 'peaks') and the final moments of an experience (the 'end') are heavily weighted in our mental calculus.[16]
>
> Lexie Kane

Considering this psychological heuristic, I typically include this emotion-triggering section near the end of a pitch document in order to try and create a more lasting impression with the reader, offering anywhere between three to six magic moments to avoid ambiguity or bloating.

Let's take a quick look at some potential examples of magic moments in existing CVCs (see Table 4.8):

Table 4.8 Magic Moment Examples

CVC (A–Z)	Magic Moment Example
Dark Souls	As you cautiously explore the dark, narrow corridors of an undead asylum, you come across a disturbingly out-of-place doll with no apparent purpose. Upon returning to a previously explored location housing a large painting, you find that said item unexpectedly allows you to enter the painting – transporting you to an entirely new, vast and otherwise completely hidden location in the game that could have been entirely missed.
Fall Guys: Ultimate Knockout	After ten minutes of multiple nail-biting rounds you find yourself in the final round of the match – Fall Mountain – with just a dozen or so players remaining. As soon as the round begins, you clumsily push and jostle your way past the others, manoeuvring between falling boulders and spinning paddles until only two players close behind you remain. As the three of you near the top, the coveted Crown in sight, you take a left as the others take a right. You race towards the top and all leap at the Crown from different directions – your Fall Guy touching it first by mere milliseconds!

(Continued)

Table 4.8 (Continued)

CVC (A–Z)	Magic Moment Example
Mario Kart 8	It's the last lap of the final race and you find yourself in second place as you drive through a Mystery Box only to receive a Green Shell – a projectile that fires in a straight line which can bounce off surfaces. Nearing the racer ahead of you, you fire your Green Shell and watch in dismay as it careens past them, only for it to ricochet off the edge of the track and magic moments' are short paragraphs that describe memorable events the player would experience in hit them before you speed ahead into first place!
Tetris	Your tetromino wall is nearing the top of the screen with only a few hundred points remaining towards a new best score! A single-cell gap runs straight down the right-hand side of your board, causing your wall to climb higher and higher. Suddenly you receive a 1-by-4 tetromino – the perfect piece – which you satisfyingly slot down into the tall gap, clearing four entire rows in one swift move!

As you may have noticed, be it consciously or subconsciously, the examples provided share several common characteristics, each of which has been broken down here in an attempt to convey what a magic moment should aim to encapsulate in order to make them truly magical!

4.3.1.5.1 They Make It Personal

While less of a characteristic and more of a deliberate style of writing, all of the examples speak to the reader as if the scenarios they describe are happening to them specifically. This plants the reader firmly in the shoes of a would-be player – making the imaginary experience a more personal one and in turn a potentially more meaningful one to boot.

4.3.1.5.2 They Highlight Meaningful Decisions

Be it thoroughly exploring a dangerous environment to find a key item or choosing when to fire a green shell, magic moments should always aim to offer examples of the meaningful choices players would be able to make in your video game, because ultimately, as a particularly renowned game designer once put it:

A game is a series of interesting choices.

– Sid Meier[17]

The difference between 'a choice' and 'a meaningful choice', while subtle, usually revolves around the trade-offs they are infused with. Using our example from *Mario Kart 8*, the fact that the green shell-wielding player had one shot makes the decision of when to fire it a far more meaningful decision as opposed to if they had infinite shots, infusing said decision with several compelling facets it otherwise would not possess – for example:

- The timing of the shot matters far more because they only have one shot to take
- The success of the shot could mean the difference between the player overtaking their opponent or not and in turn their final position in the race
- The premature or unnecessary use of the shot could result in the player being without a shell when they need it more (e.g. if a red shell where approaching from behind that threatened their current position in the race)

4.3.1.5.3 They Are Unique to Your Pitch

Magic moments should ideally capture future in-game events that could only happen in your video game. For example, let's say you included the following magic moment for a first-person shooter pitch you were writing:

'You find yourself pinned down behind cover, with very little ammo remaining, as bullets fire from all around you'.

This magic moment may indeed be a moment you envisage being memorable – were your pitch to be developed. Nevertheless, as far as first-person shooters go, it is arguably quite generic and fairly universal to the genre. It does not help the reader understand what is unique or interesting about your first-person shooter pitch specifically – which is very much a part of what can make magic moments effective and compelling.

4.3.1.5.4 They Could Happen (But Aren't Guaranteed)

As each of the magic moment examples provided should demonstrate, what makes them feel particularly special is the fact that they are not guaranteed to happen but instead the result of chance, the possibility of which is created through the various moving parts of the design. They are, in short, unexpected delights that are delightful because they are unexpected.

Defeating a Goomba in *Mario* or finding a powerful firearm in *Fortnite*, while exciting, are far from memorable – let alone magical! What makes such events magical is instead the unique and varied contexts in which they occur or surprising outcomes they might produce: a context or outcome that only your video game pitch could allow to exist. If you want to offer truly magical moments in your pitch, make sure that they are events which rely on the stars aligning in just the right ways to create distinct experiences, be it defeating a Goomba to satisfyingly chain-jump across several others that have grouped together, or finding a particularly rare firearm in *Fortnite* in the midst of a fierce vertical firefight.

4.3.1.6 Player Engagement Roadmap

As I have mentioned before, readers will be especially interested in learning how your video game would be capable of enticing players to return after their first session. Truth be told, irrespective of whether your pitch is intended for eyes other than your own, it is important to consider what the answers to such questions would be!

For some video games, such as premium titles (i.e. video games you buy upfront before playing) it may seem like this question isn't entirely relevant: 'what does it matter if a player comes back? We've already made our money!' The ethics of this mentality aside, as designers, we exist to offer the people we are designing for with the best experience we possibly can – *best* being defined as that which meets their wants or needs (whether they themselves know what those are or not). Just as a chef probably wouldn't be a very good chef if clientele only took one bite of their recipes, regardless of the fact they have already paid for it, a designer's credibility could arguably lie in how often their players come back to their games. If a player only plays a game once, odds are that it didn't provide them with what they wanted, or needed. For other video games, such as free-to-play or live service video games, players are essentially the lifeblood of such products, making their continued engagement even more vital.

Ensuring that the video game your pitch would create could incite repeat sessions is something I consider to be a hallmark of most CVCs. In my experience, there are typically five key player-focused incentives that designs incorporate to achieve this – The Five Cs:

1. Collection: the receiving of in-game assets typically offered as a reward for playing – particularly if they facilitate a player's in-game goals
2. Completion: the completion of one or several tasks the video game assigns to the player – be it finishing a quest or fully upgrading a weapon
3. Community: the opportunity for players to create meaningful connections with others
4. Comprehension: the gradual and continual mastery of in-game mechanics or systems
5. Creativity: the ability for players to express their creativity in-game

The Player Engagement Roadmap provides us with a means to showcase not only which of these are present in our pitch, but also how they develop over time and when they become more of a priority for the player during their experience.

Let's use our trusty go-to, *Super Mario Odyssey*, to create an example of a Player Engagement Roadmap (see Table 4.9) in action – see if you can spot any of The Five Cs!

Many CVCs incorporate one or several of The Five Cs in a fashion that offers the potential for future expansion, be it adding new levels to complete, new champions to master or new tools to create with. Not

Table 4.9 Player Engagement Roadmap Example (*Super Mario Odyssey*)

After X Minutes	After X Hours	After X Weeks	After X Months
Jumping around and exploring	Finding Moons	Finding all purple coins in a kingdom	Finding all Moons for all kingdoms
~	~		
	Overcoming tougher platforming	~	~
Defeating enemies		Finding all Moons for a kingdom	Activating Moon Rocks – creating more Moons to find
~	~		
	Unlocking new kingdoms	~	
Collecting coins		Finishing the final kingdom	

only does this offer a video game the capacity to offer players deeper engagement over time, in turn making a pitch stronger to potential investors, but it also allows a project to build upon experience accrued in a specific area of design – if a pitch revolves around champions odds are the project would accumulate valuable knowledge around champion design.

4.3.2 Formatting

If you thought feng shui only applied to interior design – think again!

As human beings, we can be highly visual creatures, so the way something looks usually plays a hugely important role in our decision-making process, be it choosing whether to see a film based on its movie poster, whether to play a video game based on its box-art or whether a pitch is worth reading based on its presentation. Like it or not – we tend to judge a book by its cover.

Returning to the rooms analogy from the 'Structure' section, formatting in a pitch document could be equated to how you might design the interior of each room (i.e. section), be it the amount of content you choose to put in them, what content you choose and how said content is arranged (see Figures 4.10 to 4.11).

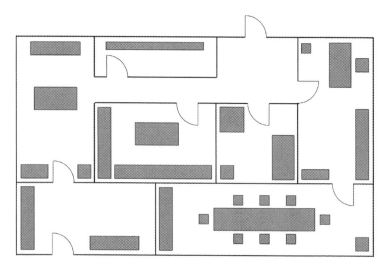

Figure 4.10 Strong formatting.

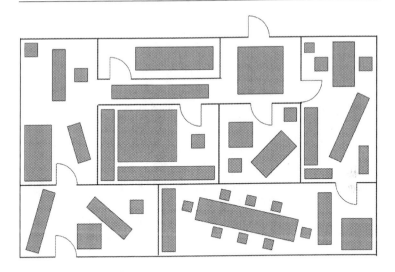

Figure 4.11 Weak *formatting.*

Considering the comparatively chaotic layout and difficulty this would present to anyone attempting to move through it, yourself included, I hope we can all agree that the "formatting" [AQ] in Figure 4.10 would be far more preferable to that of Figure 4.11! This analogy hopefully highlights what lies at the heart of pitch document formatting: making a guest's time (as well as your own) inside your pitch document as effortless as possible by ensuring it is easy and pleasant to move through, especially in this day and age where every second of someone's time counts and very few people have the time or patience for confusion or verbosity.

This is a principle that supermarket stores in particular have been known to put a lot of time and resources into:

> Every feature of the store – from floor plan and shelf layout to lighting, music, and ladies in aprons offering free sausages on sticks – is designed to lure us in, keep us there, and seduce us into spending money.
>
> – National Geographic[18]

Think of your pitch document like a (considerably less sinister-sounding . . .) supermarket store: something designed to keep visitors inside it via all available means.

4.3.2.1 Text Composition

This particularly short section offers a quick breakdown of how I have typically composed text in previous pitch documents – which includes:

- Font size: 12
- Font: Calibri
- Line spacing: 1.15
- Margins: 2.54

Stick to black or a dark grey text colour and fonts that are easy to read – resist the temptation to get any more creative than that! Between the formatting advised by this book and the content of your pitch document itself, it should be more than strong enough to grab and hold a reader's attention without resorting to Droid Sans for your sci-pitch pitch or Merriweather for your fantasy pitch.

These are by no means scientific choices – nor do I imagine that using a different font to the one I personally use will result in immediate disaster for your pitch! That being said, I have found this composition to be fairly effective when it comes to readability and visual appeal, so do with it what you will.

My only recommendation would be that, however you decide to compose the text of your pitch document, do so with user-friendliness in mind. Resist the time old temptation to reduce the size of your text or how much space it takes up on the page in order to fit more content onto a single page. As our previous home decor analogy hopefully illustrated: more does not always necessarily mean better. Ensure your text has room to breathe and avoid cramped or cluttered compositions at all costs.

4.3.2.2 Supporting Diagrams

Whenever I am writing a pitch document I always try to assume one simple thing: people don't like to read.

Or more specifically, people don't like to read what is handed to them, as opposed to what they choose to read themselves and especially do not like being handed a wall of text to read – something crammed with as much information as possible into as few pages as possible in an attempt to offer fake brevity! Whether there is some psychological principle behind this or not, I can say with confidence that previous pitch documents of my own have seen far greater success when they have avoided this mistake. Just as you yourself probably wouldn't appreciate it, it is unlikely your readers would either.

Furthermore, irrespective of how true it actually is, bearing this motto in mind can serve as a helpful reminder that every word you write is another expectation on your reader and one more favour they are doing for you, rather than the other way around. It can often be easy to forget that, however strong your pitch may be or how proud of it you are, you will very likely value it far more highly than anyone else possibly could – at least until they have actually read it – thanks to a little something known to the IKEA effect: a cognitive bias which stipulates that people place greater value on things they have helped to or have solely created themselves.[19] As a result, the reader (be it a third party or even your future self) can often end up being deprioritised to make room for the writer's own ego, leading to the reader's time being taken advantage of in exchange for overly dense information that asks them for one favour too many – which risks losing them altogether. So the question is: how can we avoid this pitfall without sacrificing clarity?

As this very book should attest to, given their ability to convey potentially complex, dense or even abstract information quickly and clearly, I am a big fan of diagrams and would highly recommend putting them to use in your pitch documents when possible to help with combating this challenge. The inclusion of diagrams is not only considerate of the reader's time and effort, but it will also help break up walls of text, making your pitch document easier on the eye and less intimidating! Furthermore, the creation of a coherent and easy-to-comprehend diagram often requires a thorough understanding of whatever information it is intended to communicate, providing you with an opportunity to ensure you understand your own designs.

> If you can't explain it simply, you don't understand it well enough.
>
> – Albert Einstein[20]

That being said, when it comes to creating diagrams, there are two important factors to be aware of, especially since a poorly made or placed diagram can be just as confusing, unwelcoming and unprofessional as a big wall of text:

1. Diagram composition: how your diagrams are put together and stylised
2. Diagram placement: how your diagrams are placed in your pitch document alongside text

4.3.2.2.1 Diagram Composition

Take a look at Figures 4.12 and 4.13 of Table 4.10 – which hopefully showcase the difference between a "good" diagram and a "bad" diagram.

The effectiveness and quality of these two diagrams can be differentiated based on their visual appeal and clarity – assuming their subject matter is relevant to the accompanying content. Avoiding the overuse of different shapes, unclear flows and cluttered multidirectional lines can enhance the visual appeal and clarity of your diagrams – making them more effective in conveying information.

It is also worth mentioning that diagrams do not always have to be branching hierarchies! With a bit of thought and practice, you will find that diagrams can be used to summarise even the most complex of subjects. For instance, Figure 4.14 is taken from one of my own industry-level video game pitches, which was designed to communicate in-game play-styles and their implications which, despite taking some time and effort to create, proved to be fairly effective at explaining things far quicker and clearer than the block of text that came before it!

Table 4.10 Diagram Comparison

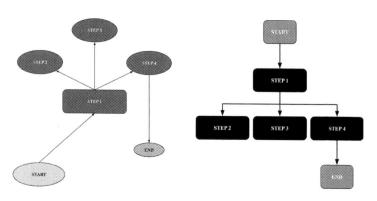

Figure 4.12 "Bad" diagram.   *Figure 4.13* "Good" diagram.

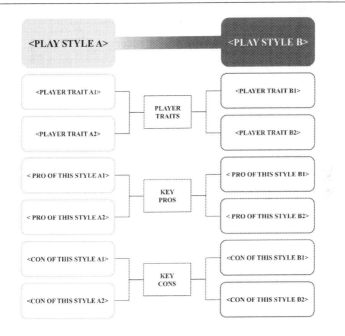

Figure 4.14 Custom supporting diagram.

4.3.2.2.2 Diagram Placement

The size, alignment and position of diagrams throughout your pitch document can also play a vital role in its readability and professionalism, as Figures 4.15 and 4.16 hopefully convey.

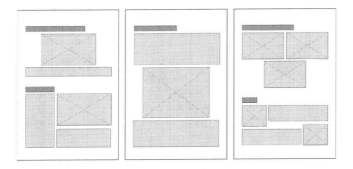

Figure 4.15 Diagram positioning – Example A.

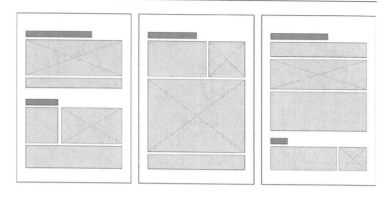

Figure 4.16 Diagram positioning – Example B.

As the second example in Figure 4.16 illustrates, try to maintain clean lines, avoid floating images or creating disjointed text whenever you are placing diagrams into your pitch document.

4.3.2.3 Sections

Imagine if this book – or indeed any book that uses a similar table of contents to this one – was just a (very) long stream of text with no sections or chapters whatsoever. The end-result would likely be a book that is far less accessible, given that it would be impossible to quickly derive what the book covers and in turn whether it is of interest to you or not, as well as a less pleasant read to boot.

To that end, I would highly advise making good use of sub-sections inside of key sections, partly to avoid the aforementioned pitfalls, but also to avoid being repeatedly side-tracked by your content. Take a look at Figure 4.17.

Let's pretend that "Section 1" offers a high-level description of the player's ability to jump in your pitch and touches on the fact that, whenever the player jumps, they generate "jump energy" which they can expend to achieve higher jumps that help them reach otherwise unreachable pick-ups known as (for the purposes of this example) "Sols". Rather than elongate this section with potentially extensive additional information around jump energy and Sols, a cleaner alternative is to simply create two new sub-sections, each of which is dedicated to these two topics.

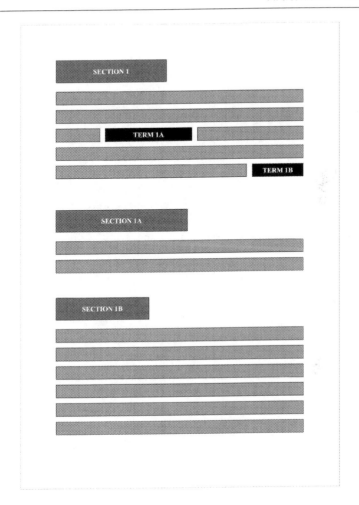

Figure 4.17 Key terms and sections.

4.3.3 Writing Style

It may be the case that you know what you want to write – but not necessarily how best to actually write it!

If so, this section is dedicated to offering practical advice around precisely that subject, an awareness of which has always served me well. You might think that this aspect of how to write a pitch document would be particularly complex and lengthy, but I am pleased to say that there are just a few relatively simple factors to be considerate of, which will undoubtedly go a long way if adopted.

4.3.3.1 Be Friendly – But Professional

It can be understandably difficult to determine how formal or informal your document should be in terms of general tone.

To clarify the previous terms 'formal' and 'informal': consider how you might write a cover letter for a job application compared to a text message for a friend and the differences between them language-wise. While the latter would more-than-likely offer a sense of casual familiarity, the former would (I'd hope!) be far more professional. For example:

- Comparison A

  - Formal: 'Everyone was extremely disappointed'
  - Informal: 'Everyone was super bummed'

- Comparison B

  - Formal: 'With whom should I speak?'
  - Informal: 'Who do I need to chat with?'

Personally, I have often found a relatively formal tone to be the most effective tone to adopt when writing a pitch document – primarily because it facilitates clear and informative language. To offer another example that illustrates this point, let's say that part of your pitch for a hypothetical platformer involved describing the unique jump/stomp mechanic that your video game will feature:

- Formal: 'Upon repeatedly landing successful jumps, players will be capable of executing a "super jump", allowing them to reach far greater heights and in turn far more powerful ground-stomps!'
- Informal: 'Players can jump over and over to get a really cool super jump that does MASSIVE damage with its ground-stomp!!'

4.3.3.2 First Versus Third-Person Pronouns

When it comes to first versus third-person pronouns, the majority of my own pitch documents have typically utilised the latter, which I tend to find reads a little more professionally and helps ensure the focus is kept on players.

To offer a quick example of what I am referring to:

1. First-person pronoun usage: '. . . my pitch will encourage players to . . .'
2. Third-person pronoun usage: '. . . players will be encouraged to . . .'

To my mind, the latter option usually offers a more active voice that puts the focus on the doer of the action – i.e., the player – which can make your writing more dynamic and engaging as well as maintain a more objective and professional tone.

4.3.3.3 Write to Express – Not Impress

Vain pontification and egotistical prose that attempts to show off an impressive vocabulary (he wrote somewhat ironically) will likely get you nowhere fast when writing a pitch document!

> Thesaurus carpet-bombings and long-winded sentences are commonly mistaken for fine writing because they feel authoritative and intellectual. But they're just masks; effective writing is lean, clean, and easy to read.
>
> – Gregory Ciotti[21]

Always remember that readers (your future self included) are seeking to acquire an understanding of what your video game is and how it will achieve that experience above all else. Avoid the temptation to try and convince them that your pitch is worthwhile, either directly (e.g. 'My pitch will be fun') or indirectly via fanciful language. The content of your pitch should speak for itself – all you have to do is make sure said content is clear and easy to comprehend.

4.3.3.4 Avoid Selfish Statements

Read this short sentence:

'Energy refills will occur daily'.

If you are wondering what the heck 'energy refills' even means then you have just experienced what I like to call a selfish statement.

Simply put, selfish statements are any terms or concepts in a document that mistakenly assume the reader will know what they mean, subsequently raising more questions than answers – when really the only question you want someone reading your pitch to ask afterwards is 'when can I play it?'

In a regular conversation, selfish statements aren't usually a problem, since the other party can immediately ask you to elaborate on whatever information they didn't understand or recognise. However, when writing a pitch document, neither you nor your readers have this safety-net to catch accidental miscommunications. It is fair enough to say that a reader could, in theory, simply get in touch and ask – but this really isn't an expectation to rely on. Every ounce of effort you ask of your reader is another hurdle for them to overcome. Pit them against enough hurdles and odds are they will simply stop trying.

Other than simply trying to be aware of them, which in my experience is half the battle, there are two powerful antidotes to consider when it comes to catching selfish statements:

1. Preempt potential questions around whatever you write
2. Offer examples to better explain what something means or how it would work in practice

For instance: let's pretend that you were describing the design of enemies in an imaginary pitch document which, to your mind, would be a vital aspect of the experience – and wrote something like this in an attempt to describe the approach your pitch would take:

'The game will have wacky enemies that make the player laugh'.

At an extremely high level, this sounds great! Who doesn't enjoy a good laugh? Unfortunately, this selfish statement doesn't tell the reader how you define the subjective term 'wacky'; how said enemies would be wacky; or how they would make the player laugh. In short: this statement doesn't think about the reader. Imagine a criminal mastermind announcing to a team of fellow criminals, each with stakes and motivations of their own, that you intend to rob the safest bank in the world without explaining how you actually intend to achieve that goal – an empty promise that is far from reassuring . . .

Don't get me wrong – you don't need to explain every concept or key term in your pitch document immediately. Raising questions out of curiosity is never a bad thing. Just make sure that you do (at some point) explain them – and ensure that those answers are easy to find.

4.4 WORKSHOP TASK

4.4.1 Chapter Highlights

- There are three main reasons as to why writing out a pitch document for your Spark clearly and thoroughly is important – even if it is intended for your eyes only:

    1. Concept development: pitch documents are an opportunity to 'measure twice; cut once' – allowing you to think through a problem before spending time and resources on various solutions. Aiming for the bullseye before you throw the dart is surely preferable to throwing it without pause!
    2. Concept definition: while artwork typically focuses on a specific area of a vision and prototypes capture a figuratively "low resolution" version of it that may fail to relay the final experience, or again only capture a small percentage of it, pitch documents are a means of not only capturing your entire video game and how its various moving parts connect with one another, but a means of communicating that bird's-eye view with absolute precision through each carefully chosen word.
    3. Concept distribution: your pitch document is a means of allowing your full vision to spread and accurately represent said vision without you even needing to be in the room.

    Additionally, your pitch document can serve as a constant reminder of what makes your experience special, providing you with a guiding star to refer back to during development wherein it can be so easy to lose sight of what's important to be focusing on and working towards. It is a way of always remembering the creative vision of what you intended to give your players – and who those players are.

- The four key challenges of any design-related documentation are:

    1. Assumption: when the content leads to incorrect assumptions
    2. Boredom: when the content causes loss of interest

3. Confusion: when the content causes uncertainty
4. Doubt: when the content fails to inspire confidence

- When it comes to the first page of your pitch document: less is more. I would also advise including four key components – as well as the Razor of your pitch (which we have covered in Chapter 2):

  - Title: While the title of your video game will more than likely change between the points of pitch document and shippable product, try to think of your pitch's title as an opportunity to begin creating an impression of the gameplay (and gameplay specifically) from the moment someone starts reading it, *Minecraft* being a superb example of this!

  - Tagline: A sentence capable of explaining your entire pitch in a single line using relatable terms. For example, if you were trying to pitch *Elden Ring*, you could say something like '*Zelda: Breath of the Wild* – for adults' – that is, a vast open-world adventure filled with secrets, special items and distinct foes alike, but designed for a more mature audience from a visual and mastery standpoint.

  - Cover Image: Invest in a professional cover image (if you can) that communicates who the player would be, what they would be capable of doing as said avatar, where your pitch would take them and what the overall tone of your vision is through style and colour.

  - Back-of-the-Box Blurb: A two-part piece of writing designed to, in collaboration with the title, tagline and cover image, quickly specify vital building blocks to the mental image that the first page is attempting to construct in your reader's mind. This includes genre, intended target audience, tone and the most unique or exciting aspects of your vision's gameplay.

  - Razor: Should you not have used the Razor to create your high-level concept, I would highly advise attempting to retroactively create a Razor for your pitch, as it can really help create further confidence and clarity around your vision.

- The rest of your pitch document should aim to elaborate on its first page's information by covering the following key sections, which by no means need to be written in this order, although I have certainly found listing them in said order to be effective once written:

- USPs: 0.5 pages
    - Three to four aspects of your vision that you believe will make it unique or interesting to your intended target audience.

- Look and Feel: 0.25 pages
    - Help your reader continue to build out that mental image of your vision in their minds by offering them a reference or two regarding your vision's intended aesthetic and gameplay feel.

- Game Loops: 1 page
    - A set of diagrams that visually illustrate the decisions to be made, things to earn and actions to master that your players will experience on both short- and long-term basis.

- Who/What, Where and Why: 1 to 2 pages per topic
    - Sub-sections relating to who the player would be in your vision and what said avatar can do, where your video game would take them and why players would be inclined to keep playing – all answered through the lens of gameplay. For instance, when tackling where, this is not an opportunity to simply describe what your gameworld would look like or its locations/lore but instead how its design would facilitate gameplay and complement what the player can do in your game.

- Magic Moments: 0.5 pages
    - Five or so compelling key moments that your pitch's gameplay could produce that are distinct and unique to your experience.

- Player Engagement Roadmap: 0.5 pages
    - A visual representation of what your video game would offer players over the course of the hours/days/weeks/months that they play.

4.4.2 Reader Assignment

1. Create the first page of your pitch document – which should be comprised of:

   a. Title
   b. Tagline
   c. Cover Image
   d. Back-of-the-Box Blurb
   e. Razor

2. Evaluate how quickly and clearly your first page communicates the intended gameplay experience of your pitch – which should be the primary focus on this page. I would highly recommend asking someone else to read it and see how well they are able to explain your pitch back to you based on the first page alone.

3. Create a skeleton for the remainder of your pitch document using the following sections in the given order and page allotment:

   a. USPs: 0.5 pages
   b. Look and Feel: 0.25 pages
   c. Game Loops: 1 page
   d. Who/What, Where and Why: 1–2 pages per topic
   e. Magic Moments: 0.5 pages
   f. Player Engagement Roadmap: 0.5 pages

4. Complete each section using the advice and insights provided throughout this chapter.

5. Congratulations – with any luck (and a bit of help from this book) you have just bottled lightning!

NOTES

1. www.beckershospitalreview.com/hr/hiring-too-fast-a-common-recruiting-mistake.html
2. https://canonish.com/problem-solving-with-kidlin-law/
3. www.forbes.com/sites/adriandearnell/2018/07/10/its-not-what-you-say-its-how-you-say-it-why-perception-matters-when-presenting
4. www.amanet.org/articles/the-lightning-bug-vs-the-lightning/
5. www.polygon.com/2014/9/30/6868309/how-to-choose-the-right-video-game-name
6. www.brandingbusiness.com/insights/the-law-of-three-syllables-that-is/

7 www.dualshockers.com/fall-guys-behind-the-scenes-video-reveals-development-details/

8. www.gamedeveloper.com/design/gdc-2012-sid-meier-on-how-to-see-games-as-sets-of-interesting-decisions

9. https://twitter.com/A_i/status/1420823405566197760?t=n__6J1ZXx0ZO WSQXDhtPTw&s=19

10. www.youtube.com/watch?v=1nYFpuc2Umk&ab_channel=TEDxTalks

11. https://vizlabstudios.com/resource-management-optimizing-the-fun/

12. https://www.taylorfrancis.com/books/mono/10.1201/9781482267334/ game-feel-steve-swink

13. https://khoa-nvk.medium.com/how-to-control-your-habits-the-power-of-habit-reviews-65cd81aa0ec1

14. www.healthline.com/health/dopamine-effects#definition

15. www.gamedeveloper.com/design/cognitive-flow-the-psychology-of-great-game-design

16. www.nngroup.com/articles/peak-end-rule

17. www.gamedeveloper.com/design/gdc-2012-sid-meier-on-how-to-see-games-as-sets-of-interesting-decisions

18. www.nationalgeographic.com/culture/article/surviving-the-sneaky-psychology-of-supermarkets

19. https://thedecisionlab.com/biases/ikea-effect

20. www.brainyquote.com/quotes/albert_einstein_383803

21. https://growthsupply.com/write-to-express/

Chapter 5

Final Thoughts

Well, here we are dear reader, we both did it. After almost two years on my part and what (by my estimations) should have been around two hours or so on yours, bathroom breaks and any doom-scrolling on social media naturally excluded, we have both reached the end of this book. A book that I will undoubtedly want to add several new topics or amendments to the moment after it has been shipped off!

Thank you again for reading what is essentially the culmination of a decade's hard work, perseverance and ever-nagging imposter syndrome around what I myself have found to be both important and effective when attempting to design CVCs. I would like to take this opportunity to offer my sincerest gratitude for your time. It has been a lot of fun and a genuine honour to have offered my personal working process as a miniscule addition to the legacy of written knowledge around the art of game design, a craft I hold close to my heart for all that video games have given me over the years, not to mention what they are capable of achieving. The power of games and play to effortlessly bring people together, from all walks of life, will never cease to fascinate me.

I have no idea how helpful this book will be to others. A book that was written across countless evenings and weekends amidst juggling a full-time job leading a new project's design and tending to both personal and family commitments no less! At the very least, my hope is that this summation of my working process and beliefs has contained one or (should I dare to dream) maybe even two insights you consider valuable that will prove useful in your day-to-day working life. At best, it has successfully communicated not only why I consider the initial portion of video game development to be pivotal in determining a video game's probabilities of success, but also an experience-proven suggestion for how to navigate this stage of the journey towards creating a CVC.

DOI: 10.1201/9781003269632-5

The preference, for some, is to set off on this *journey* as soon as possible and see where the road will take them – to jump straight into an engine and start making stuff work. Others are confident and content to head out the door with a general sense of direction. Both of these approaches and anything in-between are entirely valid and can certainly lead to unexpected discoveries and happy accidents. They can also, however, result in quickly becoming lost and confused, which can be especially problematic if the road you're attempting to walk is a road intended for team-mates to follow as well. It isn't exactly confidence-inspiring when the leader of the pack starts to look like they don't know where they are going . . .

Personally, I like to know where I am headed from the moment I step out the door, especially if all it takes to obtain such knowledge is a bit of extra time and front-loaded effort to map out the trail intended to take me where I want to end up – as well as determine whether getting there is worth it in the first place! Obviously, at some point, you have to start walking. One cannot prepare for the journey forever lest the journey is never actually taken. Endless theory-crafting only ever results in endless theories. But to quote someone who could be said to have supposedly been the first person to bottle lightning:

> Good fortune is what happens when opportunity meets with planning.
>
> – Thomas Edison[1]

Ultimately, the end-goal of an effective video game pitch is to have a solid understanding of what you want to make, why you want to make it that way, who you are making it for, how it will deliver on the high-level experience envisioned and, above all else, to communicate this information so clearly and concisely that you don't even need to be in the room – indicating that you yourself firmly understand your own directions. Information that has been decided upon through necessity rather than mere personal desire, which is often the biggest mistake I have seen in pitches I have reviewed or consulted on over the years. Game design – and indeed design in general – is not just a creative process that revolves around your own wants and preferences, but is instead a highly empathetic craft that involves attempting to identify and understand the needs of others and offer them an experience that meets those needs.

If I had to sum up the best advice I could possibly offer you when it comes to creating a CVC – it would be this: strive for accessible depth in your designs that can cater for a potentially large and currently uncatered for audience – utilising an art style that will attract said audience in the first place. World-renowned titles such as *Mario*, *Minecraft* and *Tetris* – to my mind – all tick these powerful boxes, offering would-be players gameplay that is easy to grasp while still deep enough to support variety and prolonged mastery in order to avoid repetitiveness. They are all titles that afford their players the ability to enact creative solutions within a clear rule-set, wrapped in a shell that those who are likeliest to resonate with their gameplay will find appealing. While finding such an audience may seem like an impossible task, try to think of highly successful existing video games as "bait in the water", creating easy-to-spot swathes of players around them who clearly have a specific appetite. All of my most successful pitches to-date have revolved around trying to identify big and powerful pre-existing audiences before considering:

1. What they don't currently have
2. What they would likely want
3. Creating a pitch around something they would want to play based on preferences predicted by the video game they currently "swim around"

I whole-heartedly wish you the best of luck for all your future endeavours and can say with complete certainty, should this book have been any assistance or inspiration whatsoever towards a video game you develop, that I very much look forward to playing.

Story of my life.

NOTE

1. https://proverbhunter.com/quote/good-fortune-is-what-happens-when-opportunity-meets-with-planning/

Index

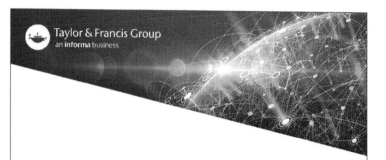

Printed in the United States
by Baker & Taylor Publisher Services